LIFE ON THE LAND

MEMOIR OF A FARMER'S DAUGHTER

*From living on a farm in Northeast Texas to
Leading Learning in Urban Education*

CAROLYN J. BROWN

author HOUSE

AuthorHouse™
1663 Liberty Drive
Bloomington, IN 47403
www.authorhouse.com
Phone: 833-262-8899

Published by AuthorHouse 03/16/2021

ISBN: 978-1-6655-1941-0 (sc)
ISBN: 978-1-6655-1942-7 (hc)
ISBN: 978-1-6655-1944-1 (e)

Library of Congress Control Number: 2021904850

Print information available on the last page.

CONTENTS

CONTENTS

ACKNOWLEDGMENTS

LIFE ON THE LAND: Memoir of a Farmer's Daughter was a thought for many years. In looking back into the far corners of my mind, I saw an idea that eventually became a dream. The dream became a reality when I finally decided to put pen to paper and write about my life on a farm in Northeast Texas.

I am grateful to my husband, Johnny E. Brown, for constantly telling me that I should write a book about my experiences growing up on a farm. Being a successful educational leader, he has remained by my side to help me figure out how to continue growing as an individual and as an educator, and I will always appreciate and love him for that. Our three children, Berlin, Mary, and Reesha, also encouraged me to tell the story of my early years so they could know more about the farm, my childhood and my family since my parents passed away while they were very young. I appreciate their endless support and that of their spouses – Desmond Edwards (Reesha) and Kyle Ruegg (Mary). I acknowledge my granddaughter, Abigail Sage Ruegg, because she is such a wonderful inspiration in our lives and a glowing reminder of the greatness that lies ahead. I am eternally grateful for the support given over the years by Johnny's parents, Mr. Lee Boyd, Sr. and Mrs. Mary Minnie Brown, his brothers, Lee Boyd, Jr., Willie, and Anthony Brown and their spouses, and his sisters Joyce Brown and Anita Brown. (Willie and Anita--deceased at early ages.)

There are no words to express the gratitude that I owe my parents and my siblings. None of this book project would be possible without the support provided by my mother and father, Berlin and Katherine Reese, my sister, Joan Reese Mathis (Jesse), and my three brothers – Billy (Jessie), Michael, Frederick (Deborah). Every day I thank God for my parents who were hard working, loving, and never gave up on their dream of leaving a legacy for their children. Anything that I am is because of the foundation that they laid. This book is dedicated to Berlin and Katherine Reese for all that they left behind. I love and appreciate Joan, Billy, Michael, and Frederick because they have always been there for me no matter what. I thank them for the memories that we made living, learning, and loving each other on the farm in Northeast Texas. I also appreciate their help in filling in details of the book where there were gaps in my own memory.

Over the years, colleagues and friends have encouraged me to share what life was like on the farm and working as an educator while also being a wife and mother. Several years ago, I met Roland Barth, author of Learning by Heart and other education publications, and he assured me that I could be an author, too. While I doubt that he ever gave me another thought, I always remembered and appreciated him for his encouragement. I am thankful for the reading training provided by Dr. Bill Blokker.

I owe much to Ms. Lee Laws, my first mentor in administration, because she gave me wise advice about earning certification as an administrator and was my first employer in educational leadership. I appreciate Eugenio Hinojosa, Doctors Yvette Richardson, Morcease Beasley, Mark Porterie, and other administrators for trusting me to do the work needed as an educational leader in their school districts. Working alongside fellow curriculum and instruction experts has been professionally fulfilling. We inspired each other to build high quality educational experiences for all the stakeholders needing and deserving our support. I applaud principals, teachers, and others with whom I have collaborated over the years. As a teacher and an assistant principal, I am grateful for the leadership of visionary principals: Bernard G. Henry, Kent Ewing, Edward Elliott, Francis Bush of Austin, and Jake Coker of Paris.

I have had many friendships that I cherish. June Gray and I have remained friends since we both attended the University of North Texas. In more recent years, it was enjoyable to work with Marjorie Cole and discuss experiences growing up in the same part of Texas. Her hometown is only sixty miles southeast of Paris on U.S. Highway 271, the same highway on which I traveled to school every day for twelve years.

Many thanks to the editing team led by Johnny E. Brown and supported by Joan Mathis, Robin Ruegg, and Thelma Dangerfield. Both Johnny and Robin are authors, and Joan was an English teacher at the high school and college levels. Thelma is recognized for her work as a member of the Lamar County Genealogical Society. Each team member offered a different perspective to editing and made invaluable suggestions for improving the book. I am grateful for and amazed at the work that my daughters did on the project. Reesha Brown Edwards worked diligently to produce a professional cover design and a photograph section that clearly captured the essence of the ideas included in the book. Mary Brown Ruegg provided the artwork and designed the eye-catching Brown Book Bag logo, which is used for other projects as well.

Last but certainly not least, I thank God for the wonderful blessings that I have enjoyed throughout my lifetime.

Agriculture is the greatest and fundamentally the most important of our industries. The cities are but the branches of the tree of national life, the roots of which go deeply into the land. We all flourish or decline with the farmer.

Bernard M. Baruch

INTRODUCTION

<u>LIFE ON THE LAND</u>: Memoir of a Farmer's Daughter was an enjoyable endeavor because writing the book gave me a chance to relive the experiences that I had while growing up in Northeast Texas – Paris, Lamar County. I loved my childhood as I lived it. However, looking back on those days provided me a clearer perspective and better appreciation of that life, which at the time I often took for granted. Therefore, writing this book has been an absolute pleasure.

The book has three parts. Part I is a description of life on a cotton farm owned by a black family. Many African Americans lived and worked on farms, particularly cotton farms, during the time of my childhood, but few African Americans owned the land on which they lived and worked. "Cotton was king" during that time; cotton was everywhere for miles and miles. Cotton provided livelihoods for many people, but most of them did not have the security of ownership. A few rich farmers owned most of the land; therefore, they determined how the land was used. My parents were determined to be a part of the ownership group. They knew that buying and maintaining a farm was a big undertaking, but they both enjoyed farming and were dedicated to making it something that they could take pride in as a legacy for their children.

Part I is also meant to describe for young people who have difficulty conceptualizing it, what growing up during the early to mid-1900s, particularly in rural America, was like. They have no first-hand information, parents, or even grandparents connected to that period of time. Many are unable to visualize the relationships between blacks and whites, particularly those who lived in rural areas. Talking with children in classrooms today reveals their confusion when I inform them that my family raised cotton and that I picked cotton. They ask if I were a slave. I explain that my family owned the land

and the cotton that I picked and that "I am older but not that old." We were not slaves and certainly not masters. As black people relating to white people, our lives were a mixture of peaceful interactions side by side with definite boundaries and separations. My family worked the farm and provided us with an environment that was enjoyable, filled with love and a sense of pride without any need to receive or expect to receive more from others. There were times, however, when we noticed that white neighbors often enjoyed certain advantages that were not available to people of color--running water and nicer schools, for instance. We wondered why we could not have the same conveniences. As children growing up, however, we worked, played, went to school, and built hopes and dreams within our world as it existed, just as children of today live life within their existing environments.

Part II of LIFE ON THE LAND: Memoir of a Farmer's Daughter is a glimpse of life after growing up on the farm. The work in the fields with the hot sun beating down on us and encouragement from our parents served as motivation to finish college and move on to teaching and becoming an administrator in public schools. My administrative work took place in primarily large school systems where some of the students did not have the same privileges and opportunities for success as their counterparts. I wanted to help effect high quality educational experiences for all children, including those who might "fall through the cracks" because their backgrounds could keep them from some of the resources needed for success. I was determined that the students I served would have high quality educational experiences regardless of their backgrounds. I firmly believe that every child has a right to a great education and that all students can be successful, given the appropriate support, guidance, and instruction. I hope that readers will grasp my passion for educating all students. I agree with Nelson Mandela in his quote, "Education is the most powerful weapon which you can use to change the world."

Part III of LIFE ON THE LAND: Memoir of a Farmer's Daughter completes the cycle, bringing us back to the farm where I grew up in Northeast Texas to take a last glimpse of the environment as it currently exists and what it means to our existing family and to the generations to come.

Note: Throughout the book the terms blacks and African Americans are used interchangeably.

PART I

GROWING UP ON A COTTON FARM IN NORTHEAST TEXAS

PARIS TWO LOVE

I love the Paris in Texas and the one in France
They're both beautiful places;
Lived and grew up in one
Visited and admired the other.

Paris in Texas had cotton everywhere for days.
Paris in France is the fashion capital of the world.
Paris at home is a place to grow up and actually thrive
Paris over there has excitement and beautiful spirits alive.

My childhood Paris is small, nice and homey
Their Paris is overwhelming, huge and worldly;
One has historical largesse and great fashion finesse
The other is home to a simple little girl in a simple little dress.

c. j. brown

CHAPTER ONE

THIS LAND IS NOW OUR LAND

The land that my family owned was rich and fertile--perfect for growing crops. My family and friends worked hard and lived life in a memorable loving, enjoyable atmosphere. The soil was rich and black, but the surroundings were humble. Regardless of lacking some material possessions, we thrived on a wealth of love, laughter, and high values. I have powerful memories of growing up living on a farm in a rural area of Northeast Texas.

The farm that I grew up on is about ten miles east of Paris, the county seat of Lamar County. Paris sits in the northeastern corner of Texas, approximately ninety miles from the Arkansas and Louisiana borders on the eastern side. On the northern side, Paris is one hundred miles past Dallas and only thirteen miles from the Red River that divides Texas and Oklahoma. Paris is at the northern end of a strip of fertile Texas land called the Blackland Prairie. The small city was home to 25,000 citizens during my childhood and was the center of one of the most productive cotton growing areas in Texas.

Once there was a little girl who heard her parents discussing purchasing farm land that was a short distance, a mile or so, away. The child was not eavesdropping but was quite ill with scarlet fever and through periods of fever-induced sleep overheard conversations about her illness and the possibility of a new home. Most of the conversations probably were not meant for her ears; nevertheless, she overheard her parents talking.

I was that little girl, and as I recovered, I--Carolyn Jean Reese--learned that we would be moving. The McDonalds were a rich, white family that owned hundreds of acres of land, possibly a thousand, including that on which we lived. Nine to ten houses were located on that property and were occupied by different families; many were relatives. Matt and Julie Reese, my grandparents, lived in the largest house which was surrounded by large barns to house mules, cows, and farm equipment. There was cotton--and other crops--surrounding the house. The house that my immediate family lived in was about a football field away from my grandparents' house. Both of those houses were located on land that was hidden from the main road by a large hill. The discussions that I heard let me know that we were going to buy a tract of land made up of about 300 acres located on the main road and not hidden behind a hill.

My father, Berlin Reese, was part of a tenant farming arrangement made by my grandfather and the landowners, the McDonalds. Tenant farmers raised the crops and paid the rent yearly without interference from the landowners. My grandfather, Matt Reese, and his sons rented the land and grew cotton on it until 1952 when Mrs. Gaynell McDonald decided to sell it. One wealthy white man, Mr. Graham, would buy the largest part of the entire acreage, including the section where we lived, for a large ranch and dairy farm. Together my grandfather, my dad's oldest brother, Essex Reese, and my father prepared to buy the remaining 300 acres.

My grandfather, Papa, wanted to buy the property together with himself as the primary owner and with Daddy and Uncle Essex as co-owners. Papa would own the largest third of the property, and Daddy would own the smallest tract. The idea of joint ownership did not work for my mother, Katherine (McCuin) Reese, who wanted Daddy's part to be a separate purchase. Joan, my sister, often quoted Mother who said, "I want each of you to work hard to have your own because when you buy something with someone else, you own nothing."

Mother expressed that idea to my grandfather, her father-in-law, who feared that dividing the land into three purchases with three distinct borders would kill the sale. Papa felt that he knew best how to proceed since he was the one who had built a long-standing rapport with the McDonald family. Mother went to Papa and told him that our purchase should be separate from his and anyone else's. Mother often entertained us with that conversation.

"Berlin's part of the sale should be only for our family," I said.

Papa said, "I thought the husband wore the pants in the family."

I shot back, "Well, if he won't wear the pants, I will."

After my mother's conversation with Papa and further discussion of the entire matter, the purchase was made as three separate transactions--one for my grandfather, one for Uncle Essex, and one for Berlin Reese. To purchase the land, a down payment of $474.00 was rendered, and the remaining balance of $4,056.50, including interest would be paid over the next twelve years. Installment payments of $335.00 were due by January 1 of each year. The down payment was paid in cash; the deed was signed and filed; and on April 17, 1952, we became owners of 91.6 acres of fertile crop land. Mother's name was not on the deed. I wonder if that part escaped her or if she were fine with the arrangement as long as my father owned the property outright without any attachment to his other family members. That was 1952, only thirty-two years after women's suffrage ended in giving women the right to vote, so making further fuss about the situation probably would have been counter-productive. I never heard my mother express any further concern about the purchase or the deed. She was happy that the sale had gone through successfully.

Once the deed was signed and filed at the courthouse, we became landowners and looked forward to moving into our new home. I was aware that we were "movin' on up" - to the other side of the hill that is. My parents spent a lot of time at the new house getting it ready for a major family move. I wanted to see the new house that they were working on.

My curiosity about the house finally got the better of me, to the point that I could think of nothing but going to see it. I was always very curious. A few months before, it was that curiosity that made me go alone to the pool—stock pond--near our house to look for a two-foot silver bass on the far side of the pool. My oldest brother had told us about the fish. During that escapade, I walked to the very end of a makeshift pier that was not secured and flipped up when I stepped too far to the edge of it. I went flying through the air like a well-thrown football to have my entire body land in the deep mud that surrounded the water in the pool. At such a young age and having no idea what to do, I grabbed a hand full of weeds and pulled myself out of the mud. I wobbled into the kitchen covered in mud from head to toe. Everyone else was preparing to sit down at the table for dinner--supper as we called it--but all stopped cold when "the creature from the black lagoon" stumbled in. My mother realized what could have resulted from that adventure and just scrubbed and scrubbed and hugged and hugged me until I was mud free again.

At any rate, my imagination and my curiosity about the house took over. I had to see the place that everyone else was talking about. It must have been the hottest month of the summer, and the doctor had said that I was to stay out of the sun because I had not completely recovered from the scarlet fever. The way I figured it, I couldn't be any less comfortable going to the new house than I was sweating all day in the bed in the old house, no air conditioning, of course. My parents were at the new home working, so I decided to persuade my oldest brother, Billy, to take me there. When my brother came into the room where I was, which was the family meeting room as well, I started, "Billy, please take me to see the new house."

"I don't have a car; how can I take you? You are not supposed to be out in the sun anyway," he replied.

"Please take me. It won't take us long," I continued.

"I can't; I'll get a whipping," he countered. At the ripe old age of ten he understood the concept of rewards and consequences. I still had a few lessons to learn.

For the record, my brother had been driving for a year or so. In those days on a farm driving seemed to just happen, especially for boys. A few years before, Billy and a younger cousin, Richard, not only had driven our old black Ford from town to our house, but while on the way they had changed a flat tire. Driving the ten miles from town to our house and fixing a flat were big accomplishments for children the age of Billy and Richard.

I had always looked up to my brother and counted on him to take care of me. I thought of him as an adult, not the ten-year old kid that he was. I begged again in my most pitiful manner.

"If you take me over there, I won't ask for anything else for a long time. I won't even ask to see your Lone Ranger funny books anymore. We can go in your new red wagon," I pleaded.

He had always had a soft spot for me, which I knew. I begged, and it worked. We got in the wagon and took off--the two of us in a little red wagon with only his peddling as power. About a half mile from home, just as we turned onto the road that led to the new house, we heard a tractor coming over the hill. We panicked, afraid it was our dad, which it was. In trying to get out of the way of the tractor, we turned the wagon over into a ditch just as Daddy and my uncle, Kermith, came over the hill. Needless to say, the rest of this tale was nothing short of a total disaster.

My dad was pretty angry because I was out of my sick bed with my young brother--no protection from the sun or from oncoming vehicles and no permission to leave home. "Who told you to leave home?" he demanded. Neither of us said anything because everyone already knew the answer.

We were in so much trouble. When we got home, my brother indeed got a whipping. I would like to say spanking, but that term doesn't seem to fit. I was scolded for endangering the two of us and had to wait longer to see the new house, punishment enough for me, added to the fact that I had to always bear the responsibility for Billy's predicament. On top of everything else, we discovered that a couple of his fingers were twisted from being caught in the tongue of the wagon when we turned over on the road. His fingers never completely straightened out, and the other part of his punishment was no thrill either. In conversations years later, Billy took pleasure in reminding me of both the whipping and the twisted fingers and my part in the whole scheme of events. I couldn't blame him.

We probably could call it even, considering that I had a few scars, compliments of Billy's leadership. Before we moved from the old house, there was an incident when he decided that we should roast ears of corn in the black iron stove that remained in the kitchen. Mother and Daddy were not at home. Billy made the fire, pulled the corn, and prepared it with help from my brother, Michael, and me. While stoking the fire, he laid the red hot eye, or burner, to the stove on the floor. As usual, I was not wearing shoes. I stepped on the eye to receive a horrible burn and a blister almost as big as the foot itself. Also, while still living in the first home, I received a permanent scar on my elbow caused by a fall from a high plank in the barn while Billy was training Michael and me to walk the rafters. We did not let our parents know about these events, scar or not. I, for one, just suffered in pain and hoped—or hopped in the case of the corn--for the best.

Finally, my parents said the house was ready and I could go to see it. I was so excited. Surely enough there it was--the most beautiful house ever.

Our very own house, painted the most beautiful white with a red roof. Our old house had a dirt yard, which we often swept with brooms made of large weeds; the new house had green Bermuda grass around it. All the other rental houses in the community with families who worked on the farms had no paint, including the one in which we had lived. The new house was glistening white with a red roof. My first view of it was like seeing Main Street USA at Disney World for the very first time. Seeing our new home was well worth the wait and the risk I had taken with my brother.

We were all excited because we had a place to call ours--our land and our home. We were landowners in our own right. Our parents knew there would be challenges in keeping the land that they had just purchased, but they devoted their lives to maintaining that land and that house. Their goal was to someday "burn the mortgage" and become the rightful owners without any chance of loss.

The new white house with a red roof was our white house--sitting on land that was our land.

CHAPTER TWO

NEW WHITE HOUSE – NEW SURROUNDINGS

I have vivid memories of our new white house--new to us anyway. Actually, our new home was quite modest, but that meant nothing to us. It was ours. The new house had five rooms, two porches, and a bright red roof. Three bedrooms were built in a straight line on the east side of the house. A small front porch, the living room, and a kitchen formed a straight line on the west side of the house. There was no hallway, but connecting doors were present for maneuvering from room to room. A long back porch ran across the entire back of the house and was as much as two feet high off the ground in some places. The area underneath was a good spot for our dog, Mike, and for storing items that we would probably never use again.

My sister and I occupied the first bedroom, and my brothers occupied the third bedroom leading to the back porch. The middle bedroom was my parents' room and also served as the family sitting room because during the winter a wood stove was installed there for heat. The living room was reserved for company. Every night in the winter I stayed there as long as allowed since that room was the warmest spot in the house, and my room had no heat. We had plenty of quilts—some with beautiful patterns--but it took a little while to get warm under them.

I don't think any of us thought about it at the time, but our house had neither a utility room nor a bathroom. Our utility room was the back porch with a wringer-type washing machine for washing and two tubs to be filled with water for rinsing. The dryer was a double clothesline that stretched across the entire backyard which was quite long and led right to the outhouse, one part of a make-do bathroom. The bathing part of the bathroom was hot water poured into a large washtub placed in any private spot we could find inside the house. We, like so many others who lived in rural areas, did not have running water. Running water was not available to us until after I graduated from high school in 1964. Come to think of it, we didn't have several conveniences that are common today: air-conditioning, television, telephone, to mention a few. No problem; no one else in our community had those conveniences either.

So where did we get water? Just as we stepped off the long back porch, there was a brick walkway to a cistern that caught water for drinking, cooking, bathing, and any other water needs. There was also a well, which was boarded up so that only the cistern was used. What was the difference between the two? A well captures water from an underground stream that flows through veins in the earth, while a cistern is made of brick and catches rain water and holds it for use as needed. To get the water, we lowered a bucket on a chain several feet down in the ground to the bottom and brought up water one bucket at a time.

In the backyard was a smokehouse that had once been used for curing—preserving--meat. We used it for storage of foods we canned from the garden. A chicken coop where chickens, turkeys, and occasionally guineas were raised was attached to the back of the smokehouse. Farther back was the outhouse. Two huge pear trees stood in the front yard, one large pear tree was located in the backyard by the smokehouse, and a large oak tree towered over the opposite corner of the yard--plenty of shade on hot days. My mother had my father plow almost an acre of land enclosed by garden wire for a garden on the east side of the house. There were two barns in the pasture that bordered the house and yard. The barns were for feeding and milking the cows, storing hay, and organizing farm tools and equipment, including tractors.

Walking around the new home was exhilarating. The new surroundings fit our needs quite well. The entire family realized the importance of the new home and the land that was ours. I remember what my father said: *This is very important--owning your own land. Owning property is the greatest thing for a Negro to have in this time. It is important that we keep this land no matter what. This is for you and your future.*

He often mentioned the importance of paying property taxes, and he was determined to pay our property taxes and the yearly installment on the mortgage without fail. Working the land was important, but it was just as important to take care of paying for the land and the government taxes, or it could slip away very quickly.

Northeast Texas has excellent farmland, which is quite black and very fertile--the kind needed for good cotton production. My father grew cotton on "the bottom land," approximately 40 acres of the tract closest to the creek on the back side of the property. The soil in this spot was the most fertile for crops. The color comes from the large amount of nutrients and minerals in the soil. On a rainy day the soil is pitch-black and smooth like the fabric of a fancy gown at a black tie affair. One sniff of the air after a spring shower on the fresh fertile soil leads little girls to make mud pies for lunch. I actually did so a couple of times—and ate them.

The fields of "the bottom land" had long rows of cotton. Guess who did the needed work on those rows of cotton? We did. All of the family members, including me, worked in the fields to complete the work necessary to have healthy crops and successful harvests. My father and my mother completed most of the work on the farm. We, the children, helped.

Working in the fields was the kind of manual labor that I was not good at. My brothers and some of my friends were much better field hands that I was. While I loved the idea of owning land and knew what that meant, working in the hot sun was uncomfortable and served as an incentive for pursuing different career goals. With education as the most familiar profession in our community, my goal was to become a teacher.

Of course, expressing my discomfort from the field work out loud was not the smartest thing I ever did. My mother, my two youngest brothers, and I were chopping cotton one July 4 holiday when I decided to "express my feelings" about the situation. I announced, "This is stupid, everyone else is celebrating, and we are out here slaving in the hot sun."

Mother responded, "You are out here working your land, so it can stay your land." That was the introduction of her speech. She had plenty more to say. Michael and Frederick took a rest break and grumbled, "If that was us, she'd already be looking for a switch. How does Cownjean always get off?" My younger brothers always ran my first and middle names together, and my name came out as Cownjean for Carolyn Jean. I did not need a spanking to get her point. Mother always had just the right words to make my siblings and me feel about the size of an ant after acting or speaking inappropriately.

Working in the fields and the sun blazing down without a cloud in the sky, I sometimes wondered if it were really worth it to pay the McDonalds the yearly mortgage installments. Of course, we all knew that being landowners, even if it were a small tract, was something special. Through the love we had for each other and our parents, we helped where we could because we were a close-knit unit. Our family quickly settled into our new surroundings, knowing this was a home that belonged only to us. The land was just land, but it was the people who lived there that made it special. My story is actually their story, too.

CHAPTER THREE

FAMILY ON THE FARM

B oth of our parents believed that owning land was important. One reason for that was that few African Americans in the country were landowners, and the number was even smaller in and around Paris and Lamar County. Therefore, it was uplifting to become property owners in that part of Texas. Owning land provided a sense of pride and security for African Americans in this country, particularly after suffering for years in servitude. After participating in World War I and World War II, black soldiers returned home viewing themselves as more deserving of better treatment. Another reason my parents were glad to own land was that it was something tangible to leave to us and the generations that would follow. Often my parents expressed to us that they would work hard to pay off the mortgage and leave something for "you and your families." They wanted to leave a legacy for their children. My father, Berlin Reese, believed in ownership as a source of pride, and he liked farming. My mother, Katherine Reese, saw having land and a permanent home as security from being dependent on others for survival. Being raised without a father present, she wanted to feel comfortable in the thought that her family had a home and a life that was safe from the control of others. Like my father, my mother liked farming as well.

My father's beliefs about land ownership began with my grandparents, Matt Reese and Julie (Smith) Reese. My grandparents came to Texas from Alabama and met while making the trip on a wagon train pulled by mules. They married on December 23, 1906. My grandfather, Matt Reese— Papa--was a tall man who walked proudly amongst those around him on the farm, at church, and any other place. He was respected by his family and by others. Papa liked walking around the fields with his cane; he was a proud farmer. He had already stopped working the farm when I was old enough to remember him, but he was always present to see that things were running smoothly. Sometimes he brought fifty-cent pieces or candy bars for us. Usually, he brought a giant Baby Ruth for the youngest of us--Michael, Frederick, and me—to split. We learned to measure carefully, as no one wanted to lose part of his or her share.

Papa was the son of a white father and a black mother and apparently looked like his father since he did not resemble his other seven siblings. We never saw either of Papa's parents, and I do not remember Daddy or anyone else saying much about them. I did not hear any conversations about my grandfather's looks or his heritage, and none of us gave his background any thought one way or the other. To us he was just Papa.

My grandmother, Julie (sometimes written as Julia) Reese—Mama--was quiet and portrayed the docile wife that was typical of that period of time. However, in private, she had plenty to say. I loved to comb her long gray hair while she told stories of how Papa and she met on a wagon train coming from Alabama and later married in Texas. As long as no one was around, Mama took a dip of snuff and talked for hours about her past and all the family secrets. She loved to bake teacakes for my brother, Michael. Teacakes were big delicious cookies with a hint of nutmeg. Michael was a big sweet eater, so she baked teacakes for him, water cornbread--cooked in a pan on top of the stove--and mustard greens for my grandfather, the best biscuits ever, and not much else. She put garlic in everything "for high blood pressure." Cooking was not her forte; her specialty was gardening and taking care of green plants. She could take a simple leaf from anywhere and nurture it until it became a beautiful green plant appealing to the eye like a well-cut emerald shining brightly in its velvet box. She truly had a "green thumb."

Mama liked the outdoors and always wore a bonnet. She was great at making bonnets and quilts. Her quilts did not have a lot of fancy designs but were well made and provided great warmth. Mama helped me make two quilts, one of which I still hold as a treasure from the past.

I enjoyed being around my grandmother. She listened to me, and I listened to her. As a matter of fact, I made my first bus trip with her. I rode with Mama to take three of my younger cousins, Delura, Ronald and Rhonda (twins), back to their father, Uncle Pershing, in Wichita Falls. I had two new experiences on that trip: First time to ride a Trailway bus and the first and only time I experienced a dust storm. One day while in Wichita Falls, a dust storm arose. The sky darkened, and thick dust and grit were everywhere. There are not enough "rags" in the world to plug up all the tiny holes, cracks, and crevices that dust can get through. Going outside was impossible, and staying inside was difficult with all that dust swirling around everywhere.

While Mama was "quiet," Papa was not. He made himself clear on everything. He was a big believer in education and learning. I do not know if he finished high school or not, but I know he read a lot and knew that education was important. He read the newspaper every day, and books, magazines, or the Bible consistently. He loved history and gave his sons historical names. Even though he was known as Matt Reese, his actual name was James Madison Reese, after the fourth president of the United States. From first to last, his sons were named as follows:

- Essex - for Essex, a county in England
- Berlin - for the capital city of Germany
- Andrew Jackson (A. J.) – for Andrew Jackson, seventh president of the United States
- Kermith – possibly for Kermit Roosevelt, a soldier in both world wars and son of President Theodore Roosevelt
- Thurman - possibly named for Senator Allen Granberry Thurman of Ohio
- Pershing – for General John Joseph "Black Jack" Pershing; and
- Calvin – for President Calvin Coolidge, thirtieth president of the United States

His two daughters, Alma and Gaynell, carried the names of one of Papa's sister, Alma, and the owner of the land that we bought, Gaynell McDonald. My uncles and aunts were known throughout the community for various accomplishments. Alma graduated from Huston-Tillotson College in Austin and became a company, later, a school secretary. Gaynell became a teacher after her graduation from Prairie View A&M University and was one of my teachers in elementary school. Essex and Thurman served in the military and later held jobs as mail carriers in Paris. One son, A. J., served as a train porter, and Pershing—same birthday as mine--moved to Wichita Falls and became a caretaker of a bank there. Calvin, the youngest son, served in the military, graduated from Wiley College in Marshall, received a master's degree from Creighton University in Nebraska and a Ph.D. from the University of Southern California (USC). Uncle Calvin taught at Wiley College and Bishop College in Dallas before serving many years as a history professor at Texas Southern University in Houston. His personal library consists of hundreds of books, most of which are historical. My father, Berlin, and Kermith are the only children who remained in the rural as farmers. Daddy bought a residential lot in Paris, but after several years, he sold it. When cotton farming decreased and industry increased, Daddy and Uncle Kermith became company employees but continued to live on the land that was theirs. They always worked at the Paris Golf and Country Club, even after they did not need the extra income. The Paris Golf and Country Club was only four miles from home and was like a permanent fixture in our lives.

My grandfather, Papa, had a strict sense of how he wished things to be, and Mama was responsible for ensuring that his wishes were carried out. He had rules, one of which was that no one should touch his newspaper before he finished reading it. Mama reminded us of that; therefore, we didn't bother his paper until he read it. He had another rule that Mama shared, "Don't sit in Papa's chair." So, we didn't sit in Papa's chair—at least not when he was around. Mama said, "Do not eat Papa's cheese." He always kept a hunk of cheese in the refrigerator, which he cut or used his fingers to pull from. We didn't eat his cheese. Maybe it was because of the rule, or maybe it was because of seeing his fingers dig into the hunk. Either way we didn't bother his cheese.

The only other rule that I remember from him was not to touch the things on the chest-of-drawers in his room. Of course, we all know that "rules are written to be broken." Papa kept Feen-a-Mint gum there. One day my curiosity kicked in, and I decided I had to try his Feen-a-Mint gum. I had always wondered why Feen-a-Mint was different from Beech-Nut, Chiclets, Wrigley's Spearmint and Juicy Fruit, Dentyne, and other favorites. I found out. My window of time was small, so I skipped reading the label on the package, which was a major mistake. I missed the part about Feen-a-Mint gum being a laxative. About an hour later, I learned all I needed to know about Feen-a-Mint gum. I also learned a life-long lesson: If you're going to disobey your elders, you best know the outcome--no pun intended.

Papa was respected in our community as a church leader, and sometimes as a community spokesperson. I had heard that he had helped one Paris politician, Senator A. M. Aikin, Jr., get elected to his office. I visited Senator Aikin at his office in the Texas State Capitol building many years later after I graduated from college and moved to Austin. Senator Aikin told me that he was grateful to my grandfather and explained, "Matt Reese was instrumental in getting Negroes to the polls to vote for me during my run for senate."

Senator A. M. Aikin, Jr. was called "the father of modern Texas education." He was a co-sponsor of the Gilmer-Aikin Laws passed in 1949 that established the Minimum Foundation school program which provided funds for state-financed minimum teachers' salaries and several other educationally related expenditures. Earlier as a state representative, he sponsored a bill to establish the Teacher Retirement System (Harvill, 2020).

My father, Berlin Reese, was the second oldest child of the family and was one of the three purchasers of the Reese land. He was born on January 20, 1911. He remained a farmer and was like my grandfather in many ways, except he was not strict like Papa. He did not have a list of rules. He did, however, speak often about the value of getting an education, especially for black people. There was another thing he often mentioned as important. My sister, Joan, often repeated Daddy's words: *Pay your poll taxes, pay your property taxes, and pay your church dues.* He believed it very important to maintain the chance to vote. Each year Daddy and Mother made Poll Tax Day a holiday that they never missed celebrating. They made a point of getting dressed up and going to town to pay the $1.50 (or $1.75) tax required for voting in Texas. Poll taxes gave you the right to vote. Property taxes secured the ability to hold on to the land. Church dues kept things in order with the heavenly Father.

Like Papa, my father was well-known and respected in the community, at church, and around Powderly High School since he and my mother had a joint bus driving job. He enjoyed being a member of the Olive Branch Masonic Lodge #19, Paris, Texas. He later served as Worshipful Master of that organization. He was a great believer in education and learning. While he did not finish his last year of high school, he, like my grandfather, read a lot—The Holy Bible, The Old Farmer's Almanac, magazines, and any other available materials. I used to watch him figure cotton payments, church revenues and expenditures. He was treasurer of the church and later became church lay leader of St. Mark's United Methodist Church, the church we attended once the four churches on the circuit merged into one. Springhill Methodist Church in the Lone Star community was our home church that met each first Sunday until the merger took place. Daddy was also church lay leader at Mt. Zion United Methodist Church after moving his membership from St. Mark's located in Arthur City to Mt. Zion in Paris. He kept a careful budget for the home and for all the farm proceedings. For Friday payday in the fields, he had all payments ready for everyone who had worked during the week.

He liked situations that required thinking and use of knowledge. I heard him say many times that he wished he had a set of encyclopedias to look up things that he wanted to know. The summer after my first year of teaching, I worked as a salesperson for the World Book Encyclopedia company. I made only three sales, allowing me to get a discounted set, which I bought as a gift for Daddy. He was proud of the gift, but I was much prouder because I felt I had given him a little something for all that he had given me over the years.

My mother, Katherine (McCuin) Reese, was raised by a single mother after her father left Paris when they were very young. Born on November 25, 1916, my mother wanted to have a life different from that which she experienced as a child which included living on someone else's property without great opportunities for education or other supports that ensured better qualities of life. She and her siblings thrived in spite of their circumstances. Mother was determined to make a better life for her family. She had to move from her home in Bairdstown to live in a boarding house on Fifth Street in Paris in order to attend high school. She sometimes showed us the house in which she lived while going to Gibbons High School. Mother was set on getting a high school diploma. In 1937, at the age of twenty, she graduated from Gibbons High School. She wanted to attend college to become a homemaking teacher, but the opportunity just wasn't there. Soon after her graduation from high school, my father and she met on a train trip to the State Fair of Texas held in Dallas. They later married on December 3, 1938.

My mother was one of five children raised by Arrie (Gentry) McCuin. Arrie Gentry married Arthur McCuin on August 24, 1907, but around ten years later, Arthur left Paris and was not heard of again for decades. He left behind Arrie and five small children. They continued to live on a farm in Bairdstown, a community ten or so miles south of Paris. Upon reaching adulthood, four of the children moved to Paris or to other cities. The oldest child, Walter Wallace, his wife, Lillie Mae, and their five children remained in Bairdstown. Once or twice a year, Mother took us to the very small farming community where she grew up. She told us about her relatives, many of whom still lived there until the time when there was a mass exodus from all the rural areas to Paris and other towns. Jim Nella, the second oldest child and her family moved to Littlefield in West Texas to pick cotton and remained there. Mother was the third and middle child. Arthur, the fourth child--named after their father-- and his family moved to Phoenix, Arizona, after living in Paris for a few years. Grandmother Arrie moved to Phoenix to live with them. Mother visited Uncle Son, as we called him, and my grandmother, but my siblings and I did not see Grandmother again until thirteen years later when she returned to Texas to live with Aunt Jim—Jim Nella--and her family in Littlefield. Mother's youngest sibling, Addie--Auntie to us--moved to live in Milwaukee, Wisconsin.

My grandmother lived with us for a brief period prior to leaving for Phoenix to live with Uncle Son and Aunt Lorenza. She did not own a home of her own. Of the short time that she stayed with us before we moved into the white house with the red roof, my greatest memory of her was that she baked scrumptious blackberry pies. She did not use the gas oven that had been placed in the kitchen but relied on the old black, iron wood stove that had been there for years.

It was amazing when years later Aunt Jim and family brought Grandmother from West Texas to visit us. Grandmother was approaching ninety years old and weighed not an ounce over ninety pounds. She was only four feet tall. My mother and her siblings were of average size. We ran to my mother and yelled, "What happened to her? What made her shrink?"

Mother thought our question funny and answered, "She didn't shrink; you grew. She was always little." Her size did not match our memories of her. Her size did not reflect any of the stories that had been told of her and how she took care of five children in the absence of their father.

Like her mother, our mother learned to work hard for her children. She was glad to have control of the land on which we lived and always expressed determination to create a nice home for her children. She worked in the fields, cooked three meals a day, raised and preserved much of the food that we consumed, and carried out many other tasks that were a part of farm life. Mother milked the cows most of the time, as my father could never get as much milk from Daisy and the other cows as Mother could. The cows liked her milking technique better—I think. Some of the milk she prepared for selling, and the rest she kept for our use at home. Mother was an excellent seamstress, making many of the clothes that I wore. In addition to all the work on the farm, starting while I was in second grade, she and my dad drove a school bus route to Powderly High School. She was a very busy person but never seemed to mind.

Mother made sure we understood that we were to always maintain integrity and high levels of character. She believed that we should be kind to others and treat all people fairly. She always said that she would stand up for us if we were not treated fairly but would not support our doing wrong. She said, "You are as good as anyone, even presidents or kings and queens. But remember you are no better than anyone." President Barack Obama made the same comment, minus the part about presidents and royalty, in his speech during the 2020 Democratic National Convention. Mother paraphrased a quote by George Washington Carver when she said, "Do the common thing in the uncommon way." She wanted us to excel in our tasks but always remain respectful of others. The complete quote was as follows: *When you can do the common things of life in an uncommon way, you will command the attention of the world.*

Both of my parents were proud of their children and worked very hard to provide for us. There were five children in the Berlin and Katherine Reese family. Joan--born on December 18, 1939--is the oldest. My brother, Billy Joe--born on July 28, 1941--is the second oldest child. He is now deceased. I, Carolyn Jean, hold the spot of middle child, birthdate January 23, 1947. Michael Lee--birthdate November 8, 1948—is the fourth child. Frederick Donald--born on May 20, 1951--is the youngest of the five children. Two other children were born into the family--Lewis Edward on November 6, 1943, and a baby girl on June 17, 1953. They gained their angel wings at birth or soon afterward.

My grandparents, Matt and Julie Reese, Uncle Kermith, and Aunt June made up our extended family. Kermith and June lived with Papa and Mama, and Kermith completed all of the work required for having a thriving farm and successful cotton crops on Papa's land. Both he and June worked many days and hours at the Paris Golf and Country Club; my father worked there part-time. Aunt June became a skilled cook, preparing meals for the club members, and we were glad to reap the benefits when she brought food home or prepared a meal for us on one of her days off. Her cakes and pies were the most delicious desserts imaginable. When they became old enough, Billy, Michael, and Frederick, supplemented their income working at the golf club.

My entire family had a lot of responsibility in maintaining the farm, but we also had a lot of support from immediate and extended family members. Everyone in my family worked together to ensure that the farm was taken care of. My siblings and I somehow became the center of attention for the Reeses. Maybe that was because we were the largest group, or because we were the only Reese family that stayed in the country. Maybe it was because we did well in school and were involved in many activities at school, church, and the community. We might have received attention because we were probably "the poorest bunch."

Nevertheless, we spent a lot of time working together as a family because it took all of us to keep the farm running smoothly. Cotton was a demanding crop.

CHAPTER FOUR

FARMING WHEN "COTTON WAS KING"

Running a farm is demanding work, and it took everyone pitching in to complete all the tasks required to run the farm and to have the funds needed to make the mortgage payment each year. I helped my mother with keeping the garden clean and weed free. Often, she and I worked after school to plant seeds, remove the grass and weeds with hoes, and keep the large garden healthy to produce the fruits and vegetables that were prepared for food throughout each year. I also helped with the flower garden that ran the entire length of the vegetable garden. There were petunias, periwinkles, zinnias, and other beautiful flowers that adorned the yard area. I loved to weed and water the flowers and later pick bouquets for the house. I suppose that I—like Mama--preferred outside work to housework. My sister, Joan, helped inside with cleaning, cooking, and other housekeeping chores much more than I did. My brothers helped my father complete the work related to the crops and the cattle. My oldest brother, Billy, learned to plow, shred, and care for the animals like an adult.

My parents were the main forces behind getting the farmwork done. My father was very strong, but I hated to see him guide the mules in plowing the garden, as no tractor could get through the gates to that area. Using mules and his own strength were necessary for that job. Fortunately, the garden covered only about an acre of land.

Our farm also produced some of our meat. Daddy, Uncle Kermith, and my brother, Billy, slaughtered a hog each year, which provided much of our meat until the next year. I was not a great pork eater, but I loved the sausage. The scent of well-seasoned sausage and the aroma of fresh coffee every morning right around Thanksgiving was so invigorating. Mother made a pot of coffee every morning to drink only one cup. No one else in the family drank coffee until years later.

Cows were raised for milk, which we drank, and butter, which we churned from the cream on the milk. Cows were also raised and sold at auction. Thursday was auction day, and occasionally during the year, my dad carried calves to Paris to sell. Cows were also family pets and had names; Daisy was the family favorite. Most of the beef for our meals was bought at the market. We bought beef in bulk and stored it in the freezer once we acquired a deep freezer. The freezer eliminated the need for a lot of storage and canning of fruits and vegetables in jars. Blanching and bagging for freezing food was much, much easier than the long, hot canning process. I loved that freezer because it greatly reduced my job of washing jars for canning. I couldn't have been happier about that new appliance. Inventions were welcome in our house. Next came a black and white television, then a telephone, and later a window fan air-conditioner. What a change! More reasons to work hard in order to have successful cotton crops each year.

We had cattle, but it was cotton that dominated. We worked on the land when we were not in school. While we were still going to school during the spring months, my father worked alone to plow, plant, and nourish the soil in whatever way was needed. He seemed to know exactly when and what to do. He knew when to plow, when to plant, and when and how to harvest. Some of his information came from the Farmer's Almanac, but the rest seemed to be a part of who he was. I assume much of it came from growing up on a farm. Luckily, we had tractors because doing that type of labor by mule and brute strength, as had been the case in earlier years, was very difficult.

"King Cotton" determined the yearly school calendar. Our daily and yearly schedules were primarily determined by and coincided with the needs of the cotton crops. The work for many people in our school and community began when the school year ended in May. One of the biggest cotton farmers in Lamar County was also the Powderly school board president for many years. He was the owner of hundreds and hundreds of acres of cotton in the Slate Shoals area, one of our school communities. Many of the families and students of Powderly High School lived on his land and cared for his cotton crops. The families who lived on his land chopped his cotton beginning when school ended in May. Their work was needed most during the fall harvest season for picking cotton, so a split school schedule worked for those families and for our family as well since we, too, had cotton to pick. For cotton farmers there were two seasons: Chopping cotton and picking cotton.

Chopping Cotton. In June chopping cotton was needed to either "weed out" cotton sprouts that were too thick for healthy growth or to remove weeds and grass that could damage the cotton plants. My dad drove to neighboring communities to pick up any persons who wanted to work in our fields. The persons who chopped cotton were adults or at least high school age. Small children did not have enough strength and stamina to chop cotton for ten hours a day. Daddy arrived in the fields with the crews promptly at 7:00 a.m. They worked until 12:00 p.m., had a lunch, water, and rest break until 1:00 when everyone started chopping again, ending at 6:00 sharp. Everyone created his or her own privacy arrangements, as there were no facilities. The crews of ten or more people worked ten hours per day for $1.00 per hour totaling $10.00 per day and $50.00 per week. Friday was payday. That was the pattern for the month of June.

The new school year began about mid-July and continued for a six-week period, possibly longer if the crops were not ready for harvest. Summer school closed after the first six weeks, or after seven to eight weeks, depending on the stage of development of the crops. Summer school was fine except for one thing: the intense heat. Just as we had no central heat, we also had no central air-conditioning, just windows to open. We also had no lunch service, and none of us bothered to bring lunches. There was a store on the corner of U.S. Highway 271 and the Slate Shoals road on the same side of the highway as the school. We "slipped" over there to buy bologna and bread to make sandwiches. That ended when the store closed for good. Starting each day at least thirty minutes earlier and dismissing one and one-half hour earlier than in the regular session gave a small amount of relief from the heat and from having no lunch. Summer school closed after six to eight weeks so that students could pick cotton on various farms in the area.

Picking Cotton. The fall field work of picking cotton began around the beginning of September when the crops were ready for harvesting. Cotton picking in the '40s and '50s was actually pulling bolls from the stalk with the cotton inside instead of "picking" the white cotton from the boll. The gin machinery was advanced enough to separate the cotton from the bolls, making the picking process easier for the field hands. There were times when teachers, the school principal, and anyone else wanting to earn extra money picked cotton in our fields. Some of the persons who showed up in the fields simply wanted to be a part of the group.

The daily picking schedule was flexible and quite different from the strict spring chopping schedule for two reasons. First, the starting time depended on the dryness of the plants; cotton could not be picked until the sun dried it from the morning dew. Wet cotton was hard to handle and got moldy just like wet clothing, causing a reduction in value. Secondly, the pay for working depended solely on the amount picked. Therefore, everyone's schedule was flexible. The people who worked usually provided their own transportation and arrived at times convenient to them. Lunch time was around 12:00 p.m. or so, depending on the desires of those doing the work. The lunch break was about thirty minutes long. The day's ending time depended on watching the sun and the tiredness of the helpers; the time was not a strict one but didn't go past 5:30 or 6:00 p.m. There were helpers who worked other jobs but picked cotton afterward to earn extra pay. Some worked a few hours on Saturday to supplement their incomes; the schedules fit the needs of the helpers. Strict work times were not necessary since payment was earned by the amount of cotton picked, not by the time put in. Some people picked a lot, weighed in on the scales often, and, of course, made more money. Others, especially small children picked small amounts. I, for one, did not pick as much as others my age, but I did okay. I always tried to pick at least 200 pounds per day but seldom met that goal. The hot sun, the heavy cotton sacks, and the long hours did not work very well for me. Further into autumn the temperatures, however, became comfortable. Actually, toward the end of the season, the early morning temperatures could fall into the cold range. Gloves were needed for protecting the hands from the cotton burrs as well as the cold. The day that I liked best was Friday - payday! The pay was anywhere from $.29 to $.33, or more, for a set number of pounds, depending on the year's cotton market. Friday was also the day before Saturday, when we usually went to town to shop, see a movie, or spend the time as we chose.

After finishing harvesting my father's crops, the workers, including me, worked in the fields of my grandfather, Matt Reese. That pattern of work was followed each year. All the crops were harvested and taken to the gin in Paris to sell. Each wagonload of cotton was processed into a bale of 500 lbs. The income gained paid the yearly mortgage and provided the revenue for new farm equipment or any other needs required for maintaining the land. Most of the years we were blessed to have successful crops and were thankful that the year's hard work paid off. Near the end of October, we returned to school to complete the school year.

Both of my parents were familiar with hard work. My mother's life, however, included more uncertainty because her father had not been present in their home since she was a young child. She often wondered where and how he was.

CHAPTER FIVE

REMEMBERING A DIFFICULT PAST

My mother, Katherine Reese, often said that her five children were what she lived for. The hard work and devotion by both parents showed what we meant to them and how much they loved us. Activities which we enjoyed as a family came with the hard work. For example, we enjoyed picnics and special dinners. One special picnic that included only our immediate family was held at the Denison Dam. This location became a popular picnic area for families from Denison and nearby towns. My dad showed Billy, Michael, and Frederick swimming techniques. Daddy swam well in multiple positions. My mother cooked a lot of food: chicken and everything to go with it. I don't remember another picnic occurring there, but I remember that one as if it happened yesterday. Mother sometimes made ice cream, a favorite family treat. No quick recipes; she cooked the ice cream mixture, and my brothers turned the crank of the ice cream freezer. The freezer had a little rust on it, but it was trustworthy and yielded a frozen dessert that was as smooth as silk. My brothers loved the Sundays when she made the custard just before time to leave for church. They volunteered to stay behind and have everything ready by the time we returned home. Everyone knew that three people were not needed for freezing ice cream, but they were happy to oblige. They sneaked ice cream from the freezer bucket long before we returned home from a church service that they were more than happy to miss.

Mother was my hairdresser along with all her other tasks. She pressed and curled my hair. Her skills in this area "were limited" I'll say, and my hair was not the most cooperative. I lost all of my hair in my earlier illness, and it grew back with a changed, coarser texture. As you might imagine, the "Black is Beautiful" natural hairstyles hadn't hit the fashion world in 1952. The task of pressing and curling my hair was long and arduous, or so it seemed, but It was good conversation time. It was during those sessions that Mother explained why she would not go onto the Paris fairgrounds where both the yearly carnival and the rodeo were held. She liked to involve us in events that we enjoyed, but she drew the line at the fairgrounds gate. Her reason for staying away from the site follows an explanation of the part the fairgrounds played in the lives of people who lived in and around Paris.

The County Fair was a huge, annual event held at the Paris Fairgrounds on the north side of the city. There was a carnival, or midway, for games and rides. Booths were set up in exhibit halls for judging many farm products, such as canned fruits and vegetables, livestock, hand-sewn items--quilts, doilies, aprons, pillows--and other wares that farmers were proud of. The County Fair lasted a week and allowed winners to move on to exhibitions and competitions at the State Fair of Texas which was held each year in Dallas. At most schools there were 4-H clubs--organizations for farm youth--that encouraged students, and even parents, to enter products to be judged. 4-H clubs were common in schools, including ours, since homemaking and agriculture were a part of the curriculum.

The fairgrounds were located on one side of the park area, and the rodeo arena sat on the other side. One night of the week-long rodeo program was set aside for African Americans to attend and sit in a designated section. We loved to see the bull riding, barrel racing, and bronco riding, and other rodeo events. My oldest brother, Billy, was always determined to catch one of the pigs that boys could chase and catch to carry home. Billy was successful on one occasion and, therefore, he had his very own pig to raise and care for. Our father liked both the fair and the rodeo and sometimes carried us to town to enjoy the excitement, especially, the rodeo.

When I was in first grade, school closed for students to take a trip to the State Fair of Texas in Dallas. Mother and Daddy, Uncle Kermith, Aunt June, and I went by school bus on a day—Negro Achievement Day--set aside for black visitors from all over Texas. I am not sure if my other siblings made the trip. I only remember that I had a great time with the four adults. I wore western clothing—denim jeans and plaid shirt--like that worn by both my brother, Billy, and Big Tex. Big Tex was the

52-foot statue—now 55 ft. tall--that welcomed visitors to the State Fair of Texas. There were few times when girls could wear pants to any school sponsored event; that day was one of those. We ate fried chicken and other good food that Mother and Aunt June prepared for lunch, and we added frozen custard, corn dogs, roasted corn, and other state fair favorites that are still acknowledged there as specialty treats. I ate far too much but had a wonderful time.

Enjoying the State Fair of Texas in Dallas was one thing, but for my mother and some other black adults enjoying events on the local fairgrounds was not "in the cards." Black people in Paris and throughout East Texas had encountered actions designed to impose fear on them during the late 1800s and early 1900s. Lynchings and other killings occurred to deter black people from leaving their work on the farms for more profitable jobs in the northern states, taking away the labor needed for the cotton market that was steadily increasing in Texas. One such event occurred in Paris in 1893 when Henry Smith was burned to death before a cheering crowd of thousands near the center of town (McNamara, 2020).

Another incident occurred more than twenty years later. Returning veterans from World War I expected improvements in treatment, especially regarding sharecropping, but were not looking to cause disturbances. Brandon Jett reported in a research project that the black citizens of Paris were upset but did not intend to commit any of the violence that was expected to follow a horrific lynching of two brothers in 1920. From Jett's findings, he concluded, "Local blacks had no intention of retaliating violently. As Essex Reese, a ten-year old black boy at the time of the Arthur lynchings, remembered, 'Most blacks had families and children; they weren't going looking for trouble'" (Jett, 2013, p. 53).

My mother often spoke of "what they did to those two brothers on the fairgrounds." Herman Arthur, a 26-year-old WW I veteran, and 19-year-old Irving Arthur were accused of shooting and killing a wealthy white farmer and his son because they planned to leave the area before paying an alleged debt. Once they were captured, the two men were burned to death on July 6, 1920, on the Paris Fairgrounds before a cheering crowd of 3,000. Jett learned—as my mother had told me—that the glee of the rowdy crowd and the dragging of the charred remains of the two men through the black parts of town were bold reminders to the city's black population of the lengths to which whites would go to punish transgressions (Jett, 2013).

A few years later when my mother was about six years old, her own father might have met the same or a similar fate had he remained in Paris. As she told the story about her father, my grandfather, and his sudden departure, I did not have to see her face to realize the sadness that she was feeling as she relived the fear and the emptiness surrounding her father's rapid escape from certain harm in Lamar County and his exit from their lives. Mother shared the following story:

> I do not know where our father, Arthur McCuin, Sr., is. We understand that a white man, probably one of the jailers, helped him escape and leave for Kansas. Because my father believed a white neighbor had misused his family, he went looking for the man. Later, he was accused of trying to harm the white neighbor by burning the man's barn down. While no harm was done to the man, my father was caught and taken to jail in Paris, accused of a murder attempt. With the help of one white man, or more, who knew he would never be treated fairly, and most likely would be killed, maybe in the same fashion as the Arthur brothers, he was able to escape to Kansas, where he remained. The men who helped him believed that he had a right to protect his wife and family. That is the last time we heard of him. Any communication may have been his last, as in past lynchings, the victims had escaped from Paris but were caught and brought back "to face justice."

> The sheriff and the men from town tried to find him to return him to jail. They asked neighbors, and anyone else who might know of his whereabouts, for information on where he had gone. They kept coming to our house to ask us what we knew about him, especially when Mama was away. The "interrogations" continued for a long time after my father, your grandfather, disappeared. On one occasion in front of the four of us, they put my oldest brother's head on

a log and put an ax to it. They threatened to use the ax on him if he or one of us didn't tell where our father had gone. We had no idea where he was.

Because of what happened to the two Arthur brothers and what could have happened to my own father is why I won't go on the Paris Fairgrounds.

My mother and her family did not see their father again until decades later when we ourselves were moving into adulthood. Her youngest sister, Addie, who lived in Milwaukee, Wisconsin, searched through records and visited with people in Kansas, resulting in her locating their father. He was doing well in Kansas City, Kansas. We visited him as often as possible where he was living a new life. He never returned to Texas, but we were happy that Mother and her siblings had a chance to spend time with their father during his final years.

As for the fairgrounds, any event on that location was a stark reminder of what could have been her father's fate had he not escaped. Such events at the Paris fairgrounds that my mother remembered and the threats experienced by her and her family made owning land very important because the ownership symbolized the kind of security that she did not know as a child growing up.

Owning land and farming were important for both of my parents, but they considered education to be just as important, actually more important, for securing strong futures for us. Our lives on the farm were intertwined in many ways with the education that we received.

CHAPTER SIX

POWDERLY HIGH SCHOOL

Powderly High School began a few years before I started my education. The school began as Powderly Colored School in 1949 as a consolidation institution that combined many "colored" schools in several communities from the entire northern part of Lamar County: Chicota, Razor, Arthur City, Reed's Chapel, Slate Shoals, Lone Star, Oak Hill, Spring Hill, Reed's Prairie, and others. The population totaled approximately 200 students in grades one through twelve and reflected many miles of roads and highways connecting several farming communities. Powderly High School was located about eleven miles north of Paris on U.S. Highway 271.

For our family Powderly High School—Powderly Colored School--was more than a learning facility. We were connected to it on several levels. The experiences at Powderly are an integral part of who I am as a person and of everything that I have done throughout my life. It does not take a school reunion to remind me of my days there.

All of my siblings were Powderly Panthers, green and white through and through; however, Joan and Billy did not attend there in the primary grades because they began school at Reed's Prairie Elementary School near our house and Baldwin Elementary School in Paris. Both of them graduated from Powderly High School. Frederick started school there but did not graduate from North Powderly High School because it closed for good in the beginning of the 1967-68 school year as a part of the integration process, and he graduated in 1969. North Powderly High School was the last name given to the campus before it finally closed. Frederick was the first and only child in the family to graduate from an integrated high school. Michael and I spent the entire twelve years of school at the original Powderly High School. There was no kindergarten, and we began as first graders with everyone's favorite teacher, Mrs. Mary McCarty. During the summer of 1952 my parents asked what I wanted when I would get well from my illness. Without hesitation, I said, "I want to go to school." At five years old I started school the same year that we moved into the white house with the red roof.

Rules and policies could take a back seat to kindness in those days. At Powderly High School kindness was the rule. Many rules that are "gospel" in today's schools did not exist at that time. Mr. W. H. Spencer, the principal let me begin school just because I got well and wanted to. Of course, I'm sure my parents used whatever powers of persuasion they possessed, and I did not want to wait another moment to start reading. I was happy to get my Dick and Jane book, which I mastered quickly. That was so exciting for me.

The only part of school that I did not like was walking in the mud to meet the bus on rainy days. The bus routes of Powderly High School had many roads that were unpaved. Our house was on an unpaved road. Therefore, on rainy days, we had to walk part of the distance to meet the bus in the mornings and walk that same path to get back home in the evenings. On rainy days the entire bus route was different, as we had to reroute the trip in order to travel on paved roads and highways. Some of the children missed school on days when it rained because they lived in muddy areas that could not be reached by bus. During one long rainy season, the superintendent obtained a mud jeep and asked my parents to transport some of the students who lived on very muddy roads to school. My mother made the regular route on the bus, and my father got up very early to make the mud jeep routes for students on roads that were inaccessible otherwise. When Lamar County paved many roads, everyone was relieved.

What was the school like? Powderly High School served grades one through twelve from 1949 to 1967. There were three main buildings: one for elementary grades 1-8; one for high school grades 9-12; and a gym. In addition, there was a separate agriculture shop, a two-room building for homemaking classes and the cafeteria—lunchroom we called it. All of the school buildings were frame, wood, buildings except for the agriculture building, which was made of tin. Each classroom had a chalkboard, a pot belly wood stove, and wooden combination desks. A trail leading into the woods made the path to the outhouses that served as our restrooms that did not have running water.

After first and second grades with Mrs. McCarty, Aunt Gaynell taught me in grades 3-4. She would have been my teacher in fifth grade; however, another school merged with our school, bringing two additional elementary teachers. One of the new teachers became my fifth-grade teacher. My sixth and seventh grade teacher was the mother of one of my classmates. I loved her classes because she seemed to enjoy teaching and was always prepared.

Sixth grade parent visitation day was a great day for me. A lot of preparation went into that special day. The teachers and students cleaned and decorated the rooms, including shining the wooden floors with oil-soaked sawdust. Powderly High School did not have custodians. Fortunately, we had Parent Day on a day that my father drove the bus. He visited the classroom to see a math contest to determine who would last the longest working mathematics problems at the chalkboard, or blackboard. It came down to the teacher's son or me as the "last man standing." We stood at the chalkboard and worked our problems as the teacher called them out. After both of us worked several problems correctly, it was a toss-up to see who would turn out as winner. I was praying that I would work all my problems and that my classmate would finally miss one because my father was there. Finally, the other student missed a problem that I worked correctly, and I won the contest. That was one of the proudest moments of my life.

That was even greater than being the elementary homecoming queen when I was in second grade and almost as great as winning a Prairie View Interscholastic League contest as a second grader when I recited the poem "If" by Rudyard Kipling. I could not represent our region at Prairie View A&M University because I was too young. I won region again in fifth grade and later traveled to Prairie View A&M University with three high school students and two teachers. I recited "The Crowded Ways of Life" by Walter S. Gresham that year. My coach, the high school English teacher, taught me how to stand tall, project my voice, and use inflections to deliver a speech to convey the author's meaning. In high school I changed to prose; I should have stuck with poetry, as I did not win first place again.

I changed to music and participated in the octet contest during my senior year. The seven other members of the group and I practiced very hard and created a bond that we knew would give us a first-place win, instead we came in second behind B. J. Graves High School, a school for students in the Bairdstown area south of Paris. We were disappointed because we wanted to do well for the principal so he could gloat at home, as the music director of that team was his wife. We had looked forward to our trip to Prairie View A&M University and to performing like never before.

I began taking piano lessons from Mrs. Inez Scott during fourth grade, and I am glad that I did. I was no good at any sport, but I played piano for graduations and other programs. Mrs. Scott was known for being a strict teacher who demanded musical perfection. Some of my sessions did not go well because I did not practice enough and the old upright piano in our living room left a lot to be desired. Mrs. Scott had a big house where she gave lessons to several students in Paris. I was the only student from Powderly High School. Her house on Second Street was listed as a rooming house in The Negro Motorist Green-Book, the publication that was the inspiration for the movie, Green Book, winner of three Oscars at the 91st Academy awards show in 2019 (Green, 1940, p. 46).

Getting to the lessons was sometimes difficult. During the summer months, I had to leave the fields on Wednesdays early enough to get dressed and get to lessons on time. Either Daddy, Mother, or Billy drove me the fifteen miles to Mrs. Scott's home in Paris for my lessons. When school was in session, I had to get off the bus on Wednesdays as we passed through the Paris part of the route and meet Billy at my relatives' house. He was attending classes at Paris Junior College and came from there to pick me up at the home of our great-uncle and great-aunt, Tom and Sammie, to drive me to Mrs. Scott's residence. After my lesson, Billy drove me home. There were several maneuvers involved in getting to my lessons, but I did not miss any. While growing up, we did not miss school, music lessons, or anything else connected with learning.

My knowledge of music became more useful during my eighth-grade year at school. We established a band that year. I had a head start in playing the B-flat clarinet because I could already read music and played an instrument, so I helped other students learn their music. Our teacher was a trained musician, having majored in music in college. Having the band teacher as our homeroom academic teacher was great. Band was fun.

Our first performance as a guest group was participation in a parade in Broken Bow, Oklahoma. We made the rather long trip and were happy to march in a parade in that town. We had practiced a lot on making the pivot for turning corners so we could march proudly, which we did. That was the same year that I started playing the piano at church. I played on first Sundays and later played every Sunday for $4.00 per week to cover gas costs. Everything in our joint communities involved a lot of travel because of the large farms and the big distances between them. Mr. Jack McCarty, church lay leader at the time, made the arrangements.

At the end of the eighth-grade year we had our graduation program and graduation ceremony in the Powderly gym that we converted into an auditorium. The graduation ceremony was nice, but the informal program was more fun and enjoyable, consisting of songs, speeches, and other talent performances. I will never forget the white dress and white spool heels that I wore to the graduation program. My mother made the dress; she chose eyelet as the fabric. It fit nicely over the can-cans, which were scratchy, stiff underskirts that made the dress stand out. Can-cans were popular at that time, but I normally did not wear them because they were so uncomfortable. The eighth-grade year was a great segue to high school. We only needed to include changing of classes for different subjects to complete the transition to high school since our class was already located in the secondary building. The high school years seemed to go by quickly toward our last and final times at Powderly.

Getting to school each day could be challenging like getting to music lessons was. A year after I began school, 1953, my mother and father became the bus drivers for our route. That meant that the family was together every day for school, making school a family affair. The long distance between home and school caused bus drivers to remain at the campus an entire day. Mother usually helped in the lunchroom or cleaned house for the superintendent, whose residence was located on the campus of the high school for white students. The two other drivers volunteered some of their time to complete custodial tasks since there was no one employed for the job.

Having everyone in one place worked fine for me since I liked school and I liked being around family. With the entire family involved in the school, our lives were centered in two places: school and the farm. My mother was the first woman bus driver that we knew of. Therefore, the superintendent put all of the paperwork in Daddy's name to avoid any questions about having a female driver. The job had been offered to my father, but he agreed to take the job only if my mother could drive, too. He could not neglect the farm work. Mother drove three days a week, and Daddy drove two days a week or on any days when the weather did not allow field work. The days that she stayed at home meant something very special for dinner--sweet potato pie, apple pie, a big cake, or something else special. After seven years, Daddy gave greater attention to his crops and put in more time at the Paris Golf and Country Club, leaving Mother to make the daily bus route and to finally become the driver of record. She drove for twenty-four years from 1953 to 1977 when she retired from the job. She drove long enough to experience the change from transporting only black students to being a driver for both black and white riders. She liked driving a school bus and loved being with us all of the time. In a Paris News article about her bus driving days, Mother said, "People always wondered why I stayed with it. The pay wasn't good, but I stayed on so I would be with my children. I went to school when they did and got out when they did, so I was with them night and day. It was great" (Vaughan, 1977).

The "anything but new" bus could break down at any time. On rainy days, the bus sometimes slid into a ditch with only the strength of the boys on the bus to help get us out. If that did not work, someone, usually my mother or my dad, depending on who was driving that day, walked to the nearest house to call the school for help. Once the call was made, the principal sent the driver of one of the other buses to come for us. On those days, if we got to school by lunch time, we were lucky. There were two other routes: the Arthur City route driven by Mr. Dirks and the Slate Shoals route driven by Mr. Ray. Our route was the Reed's Prairie route that started with picking up our cousins, the Fulbright children. My siblings and I got on next. After that, we wound through Reed's Prairie and picked up the children of all the families along the way, many of whom were relatives. We stopped in Paris to carry the students there who attended Powderly rather the schools in the city. After that stop, we finally rode all the way north on U.S. Highway 271 to Powderly High School. The entire route was one and one-half hour or more in length one way.

One occasional, unauthorized stop that we all liked was at Mr. Boyce

Reed's store located on F.M. 195. Mother would stop there on the way home after school and let us buy orange or Big Red sodas, vanilla or fudge bars, candy, or any other item for which we had enough money, usually five cents each. This store was also the only store near our home, and our parents had a running tab there to buy items as needed for the farm or for home use. Every small community in the area had at least one community store such as this one.

OH LARDY, ALWAYS TARDY! My biggest problem as a child was getting up and being ready for the bus when my father returned from picking up the Fulbright children who lived east of our house. My father always left at 6:30 a.m. to pick up the Fulbrights and came back to our house to pick us up. I did not like getting up and often was not ready when he returned. Promptness was not my strong suit.

One morning, Daddy had had enough, so he came inside to find me rushing to get out of the house and onto the bus, I turned back and said, "I have to get my lotion."

"You are not going back; get on the bus.

"I'll just get some Vaseline from your room then."

"No, get on the bus," he demanded.

"I have to kill the *ashy*. I'll get some shortening from the kitchen," I thought. I ducked into the kitchen when he headed back to the bus, only to find that we were out of shortening, but I saw the lard bucket. Occasionally, my mother cooked in lard, which was made from pig fat and was the cheapest cooking oil. I grabbed some and rubbed it on my skin as I ran to the bus.

"I made it after all," I said to myself. Later, I realized I had a bigger problem. That lard had an unpleasant smell that I--and everyone else--was stuck with for the remainder of the day. Needless to say, I stayed as far away from others as I could and prayed that no one ever figured out where the strange smell was coming from. At the end of that day, I declared, "Oh, lardy! No more tardy."

Driving down U.S. Highway 271 from Paris to Powderly High School took us by the school that the white students from our communities attended. We passed the brick building that was also named Powderly High School, complete with bathrooms and indoor drinking fountains--same name, different accommodations. We recognized the differences in the facilities, but with all the activities that we had in our own school and since we had never experienced anything else, we attended school comfortable in the love and caring that our school provided us.

Along with the studies, Powderly High School produced great programs: basketball tournaments, musicals, plays, proms, speech contests, western shows, and more. The winter basketball tournament that took place each year on a selected Saturday was a big event where my mother sold tickets from early in the morning until late at night. I was a spectator and simply watched the teams, ate hot dogs and homemade ice cream cones, and prayed that at least one of our teams--boys or girls--would win the tournament. I really liked the times during the tournament or during regular games when Powderly played against the B. J. Graves High School team because Walter Hughes McCuin, my first cousin who was in the same grade as I, was a member of that team. Jesse, Joan's husband, was the B. J. Graves coach. Having close ties to members of the opposite team made the games more exciting.

The annual musical was an event that staff, students, and parents looked forward to. Everyone in the entire school practiced the songs and other performances to as much perfection as we knew at the time. The homecoming queen was presented during this event, and students from elementary and high school demonstrated musical and various other talents. I was part of a Native American dance one year. My grandmother, Mama Julie, made my costume of brown burlap bags and complained endlessly, "You'll catch your death of cold wearing no shoes and that skimpy thing."

Mrs. McCarty, the first-grade teacher, spearheaded many of these events. Usually, one of my siblings or I had major parts in whatever event was taking place. Billy, my oldest brother, was the lead male square dancer, an unusual but well-loved event for our school. As a small child, Michael was the ringmaster in a big circus production that we put on. It was during this event that he had to say his lead part plus many other parts for students who were absent because of a downpour that cut off travel over the muddy roads. Mrs. McCarty was coaching him from behind the piano on parts that were not his until he finally turned his megaphone around to her and emphatically explained, "Miz Carty, that is not my part!" His statement was more entertaining to the crowd than the show itself. The concession man was a small part of the show but a great crowd pleaser as he repeated throughout the performance a chant that still rings in my ears:

> Popcorn, Peanuts,
> *Annnd* Crackerjacks –
> The best you can buy,
> Or your money back!
>
> Popcorn, Peanuts,
> *Annnd* Crackerjacks –
> The best you can buy,
> Or your money back!

Preparing for school programs required a lot of creativity on the part of teachers and even the students. We grew adept at decorating and setting up props without a lot of resources for such events. We learned to "make do." Plus, it was fun working—and playing--together when we should have been studying. I knew how to make beautiful carnations of any size or color from tissue paper, not to mention ribbon curls that made beautiful accents anywhere.

While we were resourceful, we could have benefited earlier from several conveniences that finally materialized for our use, due in large part to the efforts of Mr. B. N. Brown, who became principal in 1961. We acquired restrooms with running water, better buses, new water fountains, a few new textbooks, and plates without chips and cracks for our daily lunch of pinto beans and cornbread during my last years at Powderly.

Our lunchroom was far from fancy, but our cook, Mrs. Mattie Dangerfield, made the best red beans and cornbread a person could eat. Therefore, we consumed the same meal practically every day for years without complaint. We gathered in the lunchroom, received our meals, sang grace in harmony, and enjoyed pinto beans and cornbread along with a lot of chatter and conversations about everything we enjoyed--or did not enjoy. Before we returned to classes, we played softball and other games during recess time. There was always time for enjoyment at our school.

Most events were annual activities, except for basketball games and the student body assemblies that were held each week--every Wednesday 11:00

a.m.--just before lunch. There was no intercom system in the school for communicating with everyone at one time, except for a note carried by a runner or the ringing of the school bell. All students in all grades reported to the gym with their teachers for repeating the 23rd Psalm, the Lord's Prayer, the Pledge of Allegiance, and at least one patriotic song. Some of the assemblies focused on the birthday of a president or some other famous person, on African American heroes during black history week, or on some special entertainment feature—a magic show, for instance--that might be passing through town and needed an audience. Songs, speeches, or skits were presented in assemblies that had themes. The Christmas program was one such event. After the Christmas performances, the program ended with a gift exchange that included every student. Names were pulled in individual classrooms, and each student brought a gift to share with the person whose name was drawn. Each student waited anxiously to see what goodies waited under the huge cedar tree for him or her. Occasionally, a student missed a classmate's gift due to absence or other circumstances. However, every student received from the school a sack packed with an apple, orange, candy, and nuts.

Assemblies without a special theme were times for students to hear updates—lectures-- from the principal on rules about behavior, cleanliness, or any other routine topic. The assemblies continued until B. N. Brown became principal during my sophomore year.

In my senior year, Mr. Brown was the person who came to share sad news with us. On Friday, November 22, 1963, he informed us that President John F. Kennedy had been killed in Dallas. We all were very sad upon hearing that announcement. The principal dismissed school and sent all students home immediately. In addition, on the day of the funeral the following Monday, we stayed home to watch the event unfold on television. By that time my parents had placed a Zenith T.V. set in a den that replaced the long back porch. The Kennedy assassination occurred a few months after the March on Washington which we had also watched, including the Reverend Martin Luther King, Jr.'s "I Have a Dream" speech. Both events left a deep impression on all of us.

We enjoyed programs and events that would stay in our minds and hearts forever during our senior year of high school. Powderly hosted the Les Belles Parisienne Debutante's Ball—the first one for the organization--that year. The ball turned into a magical evening for young ladies from each high school for black students in Lamar County during their senior year. Our class sponsor, Mrs. Geneva Bailey, was one of the leaders of the Les Belles Parisienne Club and assured us that the evening would be spectacular. All of us worked hard to transform the gymnasium into a ballroom that fit the occasion. We practiced curtsying until our knees seemed locked in a permanent bending position. Two classmates and I were debutantes from Powderly High School. I was the queen's first runner-up, as I had raised the second highest amount of money for scholarships and other purposes. The night of the event it rained enough to fill up a small lake, but all debutantes and their escorts managed to get there. I was so glad that my father was there to carry me from the car into the gym to avoid ruining my beautiful white formal gown in the mud and water that were all over the place. After making that dreaded curtsy, I joined my escort, and the remainder of the ball was an incredible, glamourous event.

In a separate program I was one of five young ladies who were awarded $400 scholarships that year from the Les Belles Parisienne Club. Being a scholarship recipient and performing a piano solo during that program was an extra bonus to being in the debutante's ball.

The event that all seniors looked forward to the most was the junior-senior prom. And, yes, it was a memorable event. My sister, Joan, was the junior class sponsor, and that group prepared a wonderful evening for the seniors, just as we had done the year before for the class that preceded us. The decorations were beautiful, complete with a disco ball. Aunt June bought me a gorgeous dress for the event. I had chosen not to wear the traditional white formal gown, so she gave me the perfect semi-formal dress. I would never have thought of wearing yellow, but the dress she chose was the perfect shade of yellow, fit perfectly, and had the right amount of chiffon and silk. She purchased it at Ayre's Department Store, one of Paris's most expensive clothing stores, owned by a Paris Golf and Country Club member. Apparently, she described to the owner my dream dress because that's what it was. My mother bought the matching yellow shoes and accessories. Instead of a date, I went to the event with my cousins from the Fulbright family who lived near us. One was a member of the junior class, one had graduated before us and was welcome, and one was in my class. We not only were relatives but were friends, especially Erma Jean, my classmate, and had always spent a lot of time together. The jazz ensemble from Gibbons High School provided live music. That evening they lived up to their reputation as an outstanding band. One of my first cousins, James Reese, a senior at Gibbons, was a saxophonist in the group. We enjoyed the refreshments, music, and dancing that took place at our last big social event at Powderly High School. We also had fun watching the teachers--especially, Joan and her husband, Jesse, along with Aunt Gaynell and her husband, Uncle Ralph--perform ballroom dances over the entire floor. It was an unforgettable evening.

As the year drew to a close, we made trips to proms, musicals, and various events at schools in other districts, some held in the state of Oklahoma. We also found ways to enjoy each other at picnics and other small events held on the campus. I was very sad to leave my classmates and friends at Powderly High School, but I was too tired from all the graduation excitement to dwell on it.

We had great experiences at Powderly High School. I enjoyed and thrived in the family atmosphere evident throughout the school. There were many memorable, enjoyable experiences during my twelve years at Powderly High School. There were many fun, happy times on the farm, as well.

CHAPTER SEVEN

FUN ON THE FARM

Fun often had a unique definition for our family. Fun for me as a teenager was getting a chance to drive any vehicle. Billy, Michael, and Frederick learned to drive just as they had learned to swim in the pools, or stock tanks, used for watering the cows; they just did it. All three boys began driving at eight years old or so. Different story for me! Stick shift vehicles with brake-and-clutch mechanics were difficult for me, and the family car did not have an automatic transmission. One day I was standing in the backyard while Billy was driving a tractor and a trailer spreading bales of hay in the pasture. He asked me to come drive the tractor for him, and I jumped at the chance. The problem was that I was only twelve years old or so and had no clue about what to do or how to do it. I had never operated anything more than a bicycle and a red wagon.

He said, "Just hold the steering wheel and guide it while I unload the hay."

"Okay, I can do that."

I was fine until he finished and was wrapping up the task. Suddenly that John Deere tractor became the "green giant" himself, and I panicked. It would not stop running; I wanted to jump off but remembered the warning to never get caught between a tractor and the equipment behind it, so I stayed on and kept steering somewhere, anywhere. Billy saw the state that I was in and carefully jumped back onto the tractor to stop it safely. I had fun steering that tractor even though I was still clueless about driving a tractor, a car, or anything else.

While young, we enjoyed riding on a cotton bale, which was a wagonload of picked cotton, ready to go the gin in Paris where it would be weighed and sold. We rode from the fields to the house, but we were not allowed to ride all the way to the gin into town, where the weight of the cotton and the money earned were calculated.

Going into town on Saturday was another big part of farm life. My parents went to feed stores, markets, and grocery stores to stock up on anything needed for the following week. My brothers and I went to see a movie or to get barbecue sandwiches at the market on the "red front" diagonal from the courthouse where our car was parked. We used some of our earnings from picking cotton to shop at Woolworth's, Kress, and other stores to buy small items that fit into our budget. There were clothing stores, two banks, and other stores built in a square format around a big, sculptured water fountain in the center that we could visit while we waited on our parents.

The car was always parked on the street behind, or north, of the courthouse, a big granite building, that was scary to us. The restrooms and water fountains were located in the basement, and the *white only* and *colored* signs indicated which ones were for our use. The county jail was located in that building also. We went inside only when absolutely necessary. This area was called "the red front."

We spent a lot of time on the "red front" waiting for our parents to finish whatever business or shopping they were engaged in. In the early years there was a movie house across from the meat market where we could see popular movies. A different movie house allowed black viewers to go upstairs into the balcony to watch movies after the red front theater closed. Our mother did not favor that arrangement, but we wanted to see the Lone Ranger, Roy Rogers, and HopAlong Cassidy on screen. We were not old enough to understand the social and political implications involved in having to sit in the balcony. We just wanted to see the shows.

The only time that we went to the Plaza Theater, the nicer movie house located directly on the plaza, or square, area of "our downtown" was when it closed to the general public for an entire school day to allow the students from the black schools in the area to see <u>The Ten Commandments</u>. The entire school loaded onto buses to go to Paris to see the movie. Being a bus driver, Mother drove one of the buses and was able to see the movie along with the students. Following that experience, she always loved that film even if she had a little difficulty watching it because my brother, Michael, was sick and throwing up throughout. <u>The Ten Commandments</u> was my first color film, and I enjoyed all three-and-one-half hours of it. That trip was a memorable event in that school year.

Family gatherings were a highlight on the farm. Dinners, picnics, and outdoor cookouts were a great source of enjoyment. We participated in church services on Sundays where we saw the same friends from school. We went home to have full meals complete with turkey or chicken and dressing and all the trimmings after church. For dessert there was a cake or pie each Sunday, which may or may not last until the next day because my brother, Michael, loved sweets and tended to slip back often to the kitchen for another piece, another piece, and yet another piece. There were times when visitors, including the minister, came home with us from church for dinner. After dinner, we usually gathered on the east side of the house for shade and conversations that often lasted well into the evening when it was time to rest and get ready for the next day of school, or work, depending on the season.

Discussions under the stars at night about school, work, church, and any relevant topic were relaxing. We sat in metal lawn chairs and at a wooden picnic table and listened as our parents told us stories about growing up just after the turn of the century, about "picking" cotton versus "pulling" cotton, and about how they met on a train returning home from the State Fair of Texas in Dallas. We also counted stars, named constellations, chased lightning bugs—fireflies--and tried to determine where the fragrant honeysuckle scent originated from. In the summertime staying outside for as long as possible in the evening was a way to stay cool at night before going to bed. On one of those nights Michael said, "I'm going to bed early. I am going to sleep on the porch." Soon after he left us and got settled, he yelled out. An ant had crawled into one of his ears. He yelled and jumped around for a while until my mother managed to get the ant out with some kind of oil--probably castor oil--that caused it to crawl out. That night of star gazing was over.

Cotton rides, Saturday trips to town, picnics, dinners, and time under the stars made up a lot of the fun on a farm, and having people coming around provided even more joy. Sometimes our house was like that of the Waltons--plenty of us plus many others. People came to our house either to work on the jobs to be done or simply because they liked being there. Children from school packed their clothes, got on the bus and came to stay for a week or two. Evening school trips to musicals, basketball games, speaking performances, or any program where one of us was the first student dropped off could turn into a social event. The other kids got off the bus, raided the kitchen, found any 45 RPM records for the record player, and had a quick party. When Daddy was home, a visitor might stop by to borrow or return something. One word about farming, church, or politics would turn into hours of talk about any topic, including those that he told us to always avoid: politics and religion. Neighbors, friends, and distant relatives who probably were not relatives at all dropped by to discuss whatever subject was of interest at the time. There were occasions when my roommate from college visited our home with me. She observed how my parents, my siblings, and I were kind and considerate of each other and worked together to ensure that all visitors felt welcome and were well cared for.

My mother's family came at various times to visit overnight since they did not live nearby and especially since my grandmother lived with them. Family members from West Texas came and brought Grandmother and plenty of stories to tell with them. They drove nice cars and had plenty of places to go in our small community, places that we knew nothing about and only saw when they were in town. We enjoyed their company, but sleeping on the floor of the living room on pallets made of quilts didn't always agree with my back.

The family of Mother's oldest brother, Wallace, visited from my mother's old community of Bairdstown. Daddy and I went to pick them up while Mother prepared for their arrival. Whenever she could, Mother's youngest sister, Addie, joined us all the way from Milwaukee, Wisconsin. Auntie, as we called her, brought an unusual wit and sophisticated charm that endeared all of us to her.

Most of Daddy's relatives lived in Paris, and we saw them often when they came to visit us and my paternal grandparents. With only a mile between our two houses, a visit to one usually meant a visit to the other. Some of Daddy's relatives lived in other Texas cities and allowed their younger children, my cousins, to spend a few weeks during the summer months with Papa and Mama. I enjoyed helping Mama care for Delura,

Rhonda and Ronald from Wichita Falls and Sharon--her sister was born much later--from Dallas when they came for summer visits. I had often wished for a babysitting job, and helping with my cousins gave me that opportunity--for fun, no pay.

With a variety of activities and several visitors, there was plenty of excitement and entertainment on the farm. With the amusement and enjoyment, there was a constant need to be mindful that a farm could be a dangerous place. Without exercising caution, accidents and other problems could occur at any moment.

CHAPTER EIGHT

CAUTIONS, CONCERNS, AND DANGERS

Having an extended family saved my father's life one morning. Daddy borrowed Kermith's pickup truck the night before and planned to return it early the next morning. Sometimes we called him Uncle Kermith; most of the time we called him Kermit--without the *h* sound. After we left for school on the bus with my mother driving, no one else was home. Daddy drove as far as the first cotton field on Papa's land and doubled over in excruciating pain, unable to go any further. Kermith grew concerned when Daddy had not arrived as he had said he would and decided he should go to find out why there was a delay. He noticed the pickup while driving toward our house and found my father, extremely ill. Kermith rushed my father to the hospital's back entrance where black patients were received. From their work at the Paris Golf and Country Club, Daddy and Kermith knew most of the prominent people in Paris, including doctors who could perform the needed surgery. Emergency surgery was performed for an appendix that had burst. After a couple of weeks in the hospital, Daddy was well on the way to a complete recovery from a situation that could have ended much differently. Kermith said, "I am glad I just felt something was wrong and went to look for him." We were glad, too.

Both my parents believed that the ownership of land was important. Keeping the land and the white house with the red roof, however, was not always so simple. "Cotton was king" for us. It paid the bills and the mortgage. But raising the crops was sometimes challenging.

Having long periods without rain was the first concern of each year. In our area of the state, droughts could occur any summer, and a certain amount of rain was needed to keep the crops healthy. There were cracks in the ground that I used to stick my arm into attempting to figure out how deep they were. I could usually go no further than my elbow because the cracks were unevenly structured. The right amount of moisture was needed to allow the plants to benefit from the various nutrients in the fertile black soil. During droughts, my father rented an irrigation system which called for high costs and a lot of attention to keep it operating properly.

Insects were another problem for farmers. A healthy crop could be destroyed by unwanted pests in just one night. A swarm of boll weevils, locusts, or a cloud of grasshoppers could swoop in and quickly destroy an entire crop. Those pests could attack the crops and leave almost every stalk bare just as the bolls on the cotton stalks were ripe and ready for harvest. My dad seemed to have a sixth sense about danger to his crops and knew the exact moment when such danger was at hand. Crop dusting planes were always on alert to avert this type of crop damage. The crop dusters were a necessary evil, as the pilots seemed to get "a real kick" out of swooping down close to the house to leave a giant nostril full of crop dust—pesticide--and a good scare behind. We never understood why he didn't make the turns back and forth to the fields somewhere else.

The biggest fear of all was grass fires. There were times during the summer drought seasons when it was necessary to dig trenches around the crops and homes in the area to prevent grass fires from starting and spreading. One night Mr. Graham, our wealthy neighbor who had purchased the largest portion of the land attached to ours, experienced a quickly spreading fire that threatened his home and dairy farm. Every able-bodied man in the area joined together to fight fire that night. My father and my oldest brother went to help. We stayed at home worried out of our minds until they finally pulled back into the yard. They were tired and sooty but had helped to prevent major damage to Mr. Graham's home and land and to the other properties in the area, including ours. Only a narrow road separated Mr. Graham's property from the Reese land.

Maintaining the farm involved various jobs that included the use of farm machinery and equipment that could be quite dangerous and sometimes cause major injuries. One neighbor, Mr. Archie Gill, and his family moved away from our community to a location west of Paris. A short time after they moved, he fell backwards onto a sharp plow causing major internal and backside injuries. He was able to function again after extensive treatment, but the accident was a reminder that being extremely careful at all times was an absolute must.

Luckily, no members of my family experienced such an accident. There were smaller situations that caused concern, however. Usually, I got off the bus after school and headed for the television set to see what was left of <u>Dark Shadows</u>, everybody's favorite soap opera. But one day when we got home from school, we found my mother walking hysterically rocking our youngest brother, Frederick, in her arms, getting the floor pretty bloody. She thought we had lost Frederick due to a blow to the head. My dad and Kermith were repairing a fence that separated the house from the pasture. Kermith dug holes for the fence poles, and Daddy drove the poles into the ground using a heavy mallet. Frederick, toddler aged, had left the house and walked behind Daddy, just as he slung the mallet behind his back, landing a blow to my brother's head. Our cousin, Kathy Mae from Littlefield, was living with us at that time for her last years of high school. She helped my mother and Frederick get dressed for a trip to the doctor, as hospital visits were limited or non-existent for black patients.

Thank God for Dr. Perkins, the black doctor who saw black patients in Paris. Frederick only had a cut and had been knocked unconscious, but had no serious injuries. Dr. Perkins was also the doctor who had treated and restored me back to health during my bout with scarlet fever. Kathy Mae was the cousin who had watched over me and fanned me throughout that summer trying to keep me cool.

Frederick had a couple of other mishaps. One of those clearly showed he was not meant for the rodeo circuit. Our parents had told the boys not to ride the cows. Cows were not for riding. Michael and Frederick decided to try it anyway one day after school. Each of them managed to get on a cow--no experience or training, no rodeo practice, and no saddle or any equipment. How did that work out? Not so well. The cows headed straight for the stock tank at a trot. Michael jumped off and landed on two feet. Frederick, a little younger, was thrown off landing on his arm, breaking his collar bone. Michael ran into the house yelling, "His back is broken; his back is broken; Frederick can't move."

Needless to say, we ran out to see what was going on. Truly, he couldn't move, not without excruciating pain, that is. We were getting ready to leave for my piano lesson. So Mother, Daddy, Frederick, and I jumped into the car and headed to town for Dr. Perkins's office and my music lesson. After straightening the bone and immobilizing it with a shoulder sling, it healed fine. A cast could not be placed on a collar bone. The cow calamity was Frederick's last mishap. Lesson learned: Cows are for milking, not riding.

Another incident reminded us of the dangers, even life-threatening ones, that existed on a farm. One day my father was plowing in our fields, which were back-to-back with a white neighbor's land. We described his property as being in back of ours, as it faced F.M. 195 to the south. He probably referred to our property as being in back of his land. We were in school. My father, though, just happened to be working in the fields when he heard hollering--actually screaming--from the neighbor. Daddy went to see what the problem was and found that the neighbor had caught one of his arms above the elbow in a shredder. As there were only the two of them for miles around, my father, pulled him from the machine, and rushed him to his house and to emergency help. That evening Daddy told us how he had gotten the neighbor out of the shredder, removed the arm from the machine, and wrapped it in paper hopefully to save it. Reattachment was not common at that time and could not be done successfully. Once the neighbor returned home, my father buried the arm for him. The neighbor remained grateful to my father for helping him and probably for saving his life.

This incident was a great reminder that farm work could be dangerous work. Caution was called for at all times, including leisure times. My brothers sometimes created interesting activities that probably needed more thought where safety was concerned. I chose to spend much of my free time engaged in safe activities, namely, practicing for my piano lessons and reading anything I could get my hands on.

CHAPTER NINE

COMIC BOOKS TO COLLEGE

I liked reading books from the earliest times that I can remember. I was curious about faraway places and people from all over the world. Reading books was the best way to learn about people and places not directly accessible in my world.

My oldest brother, Billy, always kept a stash of comic books hidden beneath his bed. My younger brother and I were not to touch his treasure of The Lone Ranger, "King of the Cowboys" Roy Rogers, Hopalong Cassidy, Archie, Superman, Batman, and any other of his "funny" books. Of course, we couldn't wait for a chance to "check them out," which we did when he was not around. We would later ask him to read some of the books to us, which he did. He put us on his lap and read the books to us. We knew a lot about the stories because we had already done a preview. That worked well for a while, but I wanted to read for myself, which is why I asked to start school early at five instead of waiting until I turned six. I was glad that my parents and the principal let me begin early. After quickly mastering Dick and Jane, I continued to read anything with words: Farmers' Almanac, Life, Post, Time, National Geographic, Jet, and Ebony magazines, cereal boxes, and anything else. Those were the publications that we had coming to our home, so those were the materials that I read.

There were times when I was told to clean my room or other parts of the house, but I would run across a magazine, a book, old letters, or anything with print and would find myself hours later reading without the work being completed. Mother kind of ignored the fact that I had not done what I had been told to do because my parents were glad that I liked to read.

I had money of my own from picking cotton, as our parents paid us for picking cotton but not for chopping. When we made our trips to town and to the grocery store, beginning around the age of ten, I sometimes bought <u>True Story</u> magazines. I'm not sure why. Maybe it was because by that time, along with my mother, I had started listening on the radio to the fifteen-minute versions of soap operas. The stories in the magazines were similar to those on the soaps. Most likely it was the ten-cent cost of the magazines that appealed to me. The <u>True Story</u> narratives were fine for exposure to words and literature, but unlike in today's media where very little is left to the imagination, some personal details were omitted. I didn't know what to imagine at that young age, so comprehension of the full text was a little distorted. Inferencing skills were needed. Other sources of reading material were sought but difficult to attain. The school library was limited, and the public library did not admit people of color.

In fourth grade, a classmate and I began going to the school library, located in a classroom in the secondary building of our campus, to check out books. Our library consisted of a single wall of shelves that held a few novels, some nonfiction copies, magazines, and miscellaneous reference books, including two sets of encyclopedias: <u>Encyclopedia Britannica</u> and <u>World Book Encyclopedia</u>. My friend and I loved the collections; <u>The Arabian Nights Tales</u> and <u>The Brothers Grimm: The Complete Fairy Tales</u> were favorites. Occasionally, there was a book from the Hardy Boys or the Nancy Drew series that we enjoyed as well. We both had read most of the books placed on the shelves of our library after a while, so we started to repeat reading copies. All of that came to a screeching halt when the teacher who held classes in that same room complained that we were disturbing her teaching. No more library visits! I was heartbroken. During fifth grade a classmate whose mother was a teacher loaned me an exciting Nancy Drew book to read. Halfway through the book, he took it from me and refused to give it back for me to finish. I always wanted to finish that book. Years later when the Nancy Drew mystery series was reprinted and prevalent on bookshelves, I purchased <u>The Secret of the Old Clock</u> and read it, as I think that was the book that I did not have the opportunity to finish reading.

I was more than ecstatic when for one Christmas my mother gave me a Bible story book with a bright red cover as a present. I read the stories in that book over and over again. "Joseph and His Brothers" was my favorite. Since I had outgrown dolls and doll houses anyway, that book was the greatest gift imaginable. After that point, my access to reading material relied heavily on school textbooks, the magazines that came into our home, and the local newspaper--the Paris News--which arrived at our home always a day late due to a long rural mail delivery route, Route 6. Without access to the public library, eventually I ran out of new sources of books. I once ordered a series of geography books by mail. When my parents realized that I had committed to buying a new book each month from that point on, they did not favor the arrangement. Funds were limited, so I decided to cancel the order. It was not until I graduated from college that I went to the Paris Public Library to check out books. I only went twice, but it gave me great pleasure to do so since I had been denied that privilege while growing up.

Textbooks were the main source of reading material while I attended Powderly High School, and it would have been nice to occasionally have a crisp, new one, not hand-me-downs with the names of previous users and crimped pages that contained smudges, fingerprints, and notes that had nothing to do with the content. Reading from the textbooks was not always pleasing, but they were my last resort.

There were times on rainy days with breaks between school and field work when reading was a relaxing time filler. I could read for hours if I had the materials. It was my reading that allowed me to do well in college. I only wish that I had had the opportunity to read more. Upon graduating from Powderly High School and attending Paris Junior College, I realized that reading had been very important. In the beginning I was afraid to make a change from attending school with all African American students and teachers to a situation where there was nothing but a sea of students and teachers without color. I soon learned that academically I could compete with the other students, making the honor roll some semesters. One semester I failed to do so because I received a C in physical education. I didn't do well in the volleyball games. I had higher than the B average that was required, but any C automatically removed a person from the honor roll list. I discussed the situation with the P. E. teacher. She assured me that I would do better the next semester, which I did.

It was getting the required uniform for P. E. that led to a troubling encounter for me. One day my brother-in-law, Jesse, picked me up for a ride home from classes. I asked him to stop at the Sear's store so that I could get new socks for gym class. He had picked up the mail and handed me a letter from a friend who lived in Longview. She and I had been friends from the time that we were roommates at a Methodist youth camp a few summers before. Soon after we became friends, she was diagnosed with leukemia, and her letter was an update on her treatment. I picked up the socks and dropped the letter into my pocket when I finished reading it. When I got to the counter to pay for the socks, the store clerk with a wide smirk on her face asked, "Don't you want to pay for that other pair in your pocket?" In shock, I pulled out the letter and showed it to the clerk. She simply said, "Oh, I thought you had another pair." She gave no apology or any acknowledgment of her false accusation.

Some things linger in your mind like sour milk in your mouth; that incident was one of those things. I never shared the story with anyone because it was a degrading, embarrassing reminder of the fact that I had been followed, observed, then accused when I had done nothing wrong. The incident comes flooding back to me like a Boeing 747 landing on an airport runway each time I hear of a young person on the receiving end of an unjust treatment. I realized then that I was just a small cog in a big wheel that sometimes turned in the wrong direction.

At Paris Junior College I did well in all of my courses, to the point of having my music instructor talk with my father to encourage me to major in music when I moved on to North Texas. I enjoyed my history and English courses, especially British Literature. The instructor, Ms. Fuller, made the text come alive. She always moved about the classroom in shoes with heels that were about the same height as she was, being quite petite. Her enthusiasm when discussing literature mixed with my love of reading led to my decision to major in elementary education with a minor in English. I could continue enjoying reading as a profession.

In 1966, I graduated from Paris Junior College with one other African American student and an associate degree. It was rewarding to return to

Paris Junior College in 2003 to be recognized as an inductee in the college's Hall of Honor.

I learned, particularly at North Texas State University, that while I did "hold my own" I could have been much better prepared. I had a fairly good background and a determination to make good grades, both of which served me well. Looking back, I would have read more, studied harder, taken more difficult courses, and accomplished far more as I attempted to further my education and to pursue more challenging career opportunities. I found myself competing with colleagues who had much greater exposure to more complex learning than I knew existed.

While I could have made even better grades and attacked more challenging studies, I am grateful that my love of reading while growing up on the farm paid off quite well during my college years and beyond. I loved comic books; I still do. They meant more, though, than entertainment. They were the beginning of my great interest in reading and started me on a path of success in future endeavors.

CHAPTER TEN

HOW IT ALL TURNED OUT – BURNING THE MORTGAGE

As the years passed, our lives changed. The memories remained strong but with different underlying conditions. The family continued the connections to the land, our land, even though we added other experiences as the scope of our lives expanded. On January 1, 1964, my parents made the last payment of $371.50—slightly more than the other installments--on the mortgage to complete the purchase of the land on which we lived. They symbolically "burned the mortgage" agreement. The debt was paid in full twelve years after the deed was signed, and the land officially became the property of Berlin and Katherine Reese and any heirs that followed.

Cotton had been the basis of our livelihood for years, but cotton as an economic venture was becoming less important. "King Cotton" gave way to a manufacturing structure. Agrarian economies and lifestyles changed to more industrialized living when large, modern corporations, such as the Campbell Soup Company, Uarco, Incorporated, Kimberly-Clark Corporation, Philips Lighting Company, and others moved into the area and established a different economic base. Companies and businesses provided employment to many people in Lamar County who had previously depended on farming for their livelihood. "King Cotton" was fading away in Lamar County.

Farming in the rural areas decreased, and jobs in the city with consistent wages and benefits increased. People left their country homes for life in the city. My parents stopped cotton farming but continued to live on the farm. The land was theirs, and that is where they stayed.

My father worked eleven years at the Campbell Soup Company, and Uncle Kermith worked eighteen years at Uarco, Incorporated. Other than the Paris Golf and Country Club, neither of them had worked anywhere but on the farm raising cotton. It was hard to imagine Daddy doing anything but taking care of the crops, but the transition was easy for him because of all the years of being a part-time waiter at the Paris Golf and Country Club. His responsibilities at Campbell Soup mainly involved preparing and serving breakfast and lunch to the company executives. Daddy retired from the Campbell Soup Company on his birthday, January 20, 1976.

My mother continued to drive the school bus. Segregated schools in Powderly were dissolved in 1967 to form North Lamar Independent School District. The building that previously served as the campus for all white students remained intact as an elementary school, and the North Powderly High School campus was demolished. Frederick was the last student to leave North Powderly High School. He said, "I was determined to be the last one to leave our school. I wanted to carry out the last box."

Mr. B. N. Brown, the principal of North Powderly High School, continued as a principal in the new district. One of the new campuses was named for a teacher from North Powderly High School. Geneva Bailey Intermediate School was named to honor Geneva Bailey, a family relative and a long-time math teacher.

The children in my family were pursuing higher education and career opportunities by that time. My parents often discussed how this would occur--not if it would occur. They held a strong belief in "passing it on." Joan would help Billy since she was the oldest, and in turn Billy would help me. I lived with Joan and Jesse while attending Paris Junior College, and Billy helped buy books and materials that I needed for classes. By the time that I graduated from college, my younger brothers had worked enough at the Paris Golf and Country Club to be quite self-supporting. In order to cut costs, all five of us attended Paris Junior College (PJC) before moving on to four-year colleges or universities.

After this transition period, my parents were finally comfortable financially. The farm was paid for, and the five children were young adults starting their own careers and families. The city of Paris and Lamar County further improved roads in the rural areas, and running water was provided throughout the rural communities--a major change. Once running water was available, Mother and Daddy remodeled the house to accommodate a bathroom and a modern kitchen complete with a washer and a dryer set. They also placed heating in every room.

Joan--Joann to us--was the first-born child of Berlin and Katherine Reese and my only sister. She was also Matt and Julie Reese's first grandchild. Joan began school at an early age and our aunt, Sister Maggie, let her skip a grade or two; therefore, she finished Powderly High School at sixteen years of age as class valedictorian and began college a few months later. She was the first family member to attend and graduate from Paris Junior College. Later, she became the first African American instructor at the college that she helped to integrate years before. She graduated from Paris Junior College (PJC) in 1958 and began teaching English there fifteen years later in 1973. Not only was she an instructor at PJC, but the institution recognized her for outstanding contributions on more than one occasion. She was an inductee into the PJC Hall of Honor, and she was the recipient of the 2011 prestigious Piper Professor Award during a banquet in her honor.

Joan attended Wiley College in Marshall, Texas, after receiving an associate degree from PJC. During her graduation year from Wiley, she was both homecoming queen and United Negro College Fund (UNCF) queen. She received a bachelor's degree from Wiley and began teaching English at Powderly High School. She was my teacher the last three years of high school. In our small, rural community relatives teaching relatives was common. Next, she taught at Gibbons High School, the high school from which my mother graduated and the only black high school inside the city limits of Paris. When Gibbons closed due to integration, she taught at Paris High School. Joan took graduate courses at four universities, including East Texas State University in Commerce, where she received her master's degree. After a short time at Paris High School, she was asked to take a teaching position at Paris Junior College.

Joan touched many lives in Paris and Lamar County as a result of teaching at four institutions in the same area and being an active member at St. Paul Baptist Church. She carried out all her career duties while she and her husband, Jesse Mathis, reared three children. She met Jesse when he came to Paris to teach at B. J. Graves High School in the Delmar district. Jerry, their first child and my parents' first grandchild served in the U. S. Air Force and worked at the Campbell Soup Company. Judy who was homecoming queen during her senior year at Paris High School graduated from Dillard University in New Orleans, Louisiana, and became a nurse and mother of three prior to an illness that ended in her early homegoing. Jason, Joan's youngest child, graduated from Texas State University and later from the Texas Tech School of Law. He became an assistant district attorney in the Dallas area, where he and his family reside.

The second child in my family and my oldest brother, my ten-year old "partner in crime," Billy, married Jessie Ridley, and they have two children, Ramon and Monique. Ramon attended Memphis State University and later served in the military, working as a technology expert as part of his duties. Monique acquired full retirement from the U. S. Navy and later received a bachelor's degree from St. Leo University of Virginia Beach, Virginia, and still pursues graduate studies.

After graduating from Powderly High School and Paris Junior College, Billy left the farm to attend and graduate from Prairie View A&M University. Billy had natural ability regarding farm work like our father, so it was no surprise that he majored in education and minored in agriculture. He worked as a soil conservationist in East Texas before he spent two years in the Peace Corps, serving in the country of Guinea in West Africa. His assignment there focused on training the African citizens to use more advanced agricultural practices in order to yield better food crops. His training for the Peace Corps had taken place at Southern University in Baton Rouge, Louisiana, where he met Jessie. Billy and Jessie married once he returned home from Africa. He enjoyed presenting programs to describe life in Africa and his experiences there. As a performing soloist, Jessie complemented his presentations with African music.

After returning to the United States from Africa, there was a time when Billy's connection to the Peace Corps saved him from certain disaster during one of his trips to visit Jessie in Louisiana. He was stopped by a highway patrolman and taken to jail for no apparent reason. He gave the following description of the incident:

Upon questioning, it was apparent that this situation would not end well. Except for policemen, no one else was present. I had not been allowed to make a telephone call. After a considerable amount of time, I finally remembered that I had a Peace Corps I.D. and showed it to the arresting officers. That official card, complete with President Lyndon B. Johnson's signature on it, struck a chord. The officers decided that it might be best to release me and reluctantly allowed me to continue my journey. They had a few words of warning for the "boy from Texas" and released me to continue my trip. I made other drives through Louisiana with great care.

Billy assumed another agricultural position in East Texas and began graduate school at East Texas State University in Commerce. While there he met some Ciba-Geigy Corporation executives and later worked for that company in San Antonio, Houston, and finally Memphis, Tennessee, as a chemical expert until his retirement back to Texas. He then established his own business in Paris. Along with both our parents, my oldest brother is now deceased.

Michael, the fourth and the second youngest child was the last one in the family to graduate from North Powderly High School. He attended Paris Junior College before he joined the U. S. Army and served a year's tour in Vietnam at the height of that long and costly war. He was the only grandchild of Matt and Julie Reese to serve in the military. The year that Michael spent in Vietnam was the longest year of our lives, not knowing from day to day what was happening in that part of the world. To add to the tension of his being in a war zone, he wrote letters to Mother and me that suddenly stopped without closings. He never explained the abrupt endings. He simply said, "I was determined to come home without use of the crutches that others depended on. And that's what I did." Upon returning home from Vietnam and the service, Michael returned to Paris Junior College and earned an associate degree from that institution. He attended East Texas State University and worked for Phillips Electronics North America Corporation in Paris.

Frederick, the youngest child, and his wife, Deborah, live on what was originally my grandfather's land. Upon his death, my grandfather willed part of the land with the home site to Uncle Kermith and Aunt June, who willed it to Frederick and his family. Frederick maintains the entire farm originally owned by my grandfather while actually owning only six acres of it. He and his wife, Deborah, built a lovely home on the property and enjoy taking care of the farm. What they refer to as fun, I call hard work.

Frederick and Deborah have one daughter, Amanda, who received a bachelor's degree from East Texas State University and is a social worker helping young girls of Dallas. After graduating from East Texas State University in Commerce, he became one of the first African American bank tellers in Paris. Because he enjoyed helping people, he began working as a career placement officer at the Texas Employment Commission (TEC), now the Northeast Texas Workforce Solutions. He and Deborah are well known in Paris for working with the youth basketball, softball, and baseball teams. They gained several first-place recognitions during the time that he was a volunteer coach. He said, "It was connecting with and motivating the team members, more than coaching knowledge, that worked." Just as our parents did, especially my mother, Frederick and Deborah volunteered to work with youth groups at Mt. Zion United Methodist Church and throughout the community as a way to maintain a close connection with their daughter.

I was the third and middle child of the family. The same year, 1964, that we "burned the mortgage," making us full owners of the land, was the year in which I graduated from Powderly High School. The years from beginning to end, 1952-1964, that we held the mortgage coincided with the years that I attended Powderly High School from the first through twelfth grades. 1964 was also the year in which Billy graduated from Prairie View A&M University. 1964 was a landmark year for the family and me.

I was valedictorian of my class of fourteen students. One of my happiest moments was presenting the valedictorian's speech on senior graduation night. This program was an informal event that Powderly always held prior to the commencement. My entire family, except Billy who was still at Prairie View, was there. I was afraid that Daddy would not make it, but as I went to the podium, I saw him sitting in the audience, so I gave the speech that I wrote myself with great pride. The baccalaureate and commencement exercises were touching reminders that after twelve years of being together, we were about to go our separate ways into the next phase of our lives. On Friday night, May 15, 1964, my thirteen classmates and I graduated from Powderly High School.

The very next day, I went with one of the Powderly teachers to North Texas State University, hoping to get all the needed information for enrolling there in the Fall as a freshman. The teacher was preparing to take summer graduate courses. Everything was going well with my visit until I was told that there were no more dormitory rooms for African American students. "There are rooming houses on the other side of town," the registration official said.

"Is there transportation to the campus?" I asked.

"No, I am sure you can carpool with other students who live over there," she responded.

I left the registration office and announced to Mr. and Mrs. Young, the teacher and her husband, that I was ready to go home. As we traveled back to Paris, I related to them the conversation that I had with the official from North Texas State University and told them that I would return in two years. My mother sometimes said to my siblings and me that *not having all that you want builds character.* While she was referring to funds, I felt that her principle applied in this case. As we rode, I thought, "My character building got a real boost today."

I was disappointed, but my sister and brother before me had graduated from Paris Junior College, so I enrolled there in the Fall after my high school graduation.

My classmates and I went our separate ways after high school. Some of our fourteen graduates went on to college, and three of us graduated from universities. One became a teacher but passed away from illness while still young. One became a medical doctor, and I became a teacher and later a school administrator. Four classmates served in military service. One of them, Vernell Jenkins, was killed in combat soon after graduation while serving in Vietnam. His name is included on the Vietnam Veteran's Memorial in Washington, D.C. I unsuccessfully searched for Vernell's name while on a family trip there. However, I was able to find his name on a traveling replica of the monument that made a stop in Port Arthur, where my husband and I currently live. The traveling replica program had guides to assist with locating individual names, and one of them helped me find the name of my former classmate. It was a moving experience to see one of my classmates honored there.

The times working in the hot sun made me think of becoming a teacher, especially, since I had enjoyed taking over classes at Powderly High School when the actual teachers were called away for any of several reasons: a faculty meeting, to conduct practice for an upcoming program, to provide information to an important visitor, or any situation that called for a response from a particular instructor. Graduating from junior college was the first step in that direction. Getting back to North Texas State University (NTSU) was the next step, which I took two years later as planned.

By postponing my enrollment at North Texas State University, I became the beneficiary of two unexpected opportunities that came my way like a killer whale bursting through the ocean's surface. First, during the spring semester of my second year at Paris Junior College, I became the first African American to acquire a clerical position in the Social Security Administration (SSA) office located in Paris. That was a significant accomplishment because at that time there were no African Americans who held office or sales positions in any place in Paris except for a couple of small stores run by black owners in the neighborhoods where blacks lived. I finally had the kind of employment that I had longed for when working in the fields was the only possibility. Also, I was able to earn some of the funds needed for going away to college. I completed a background check, fingerprinting, and all that goes with gaining the classified status needed for government employment. I accepted the position with the understanding that I would head to my third year of college in Denton as soon as the fall semester began. That arrangement was acceptable to the director of the SSA office because the year was 1966, and it was important that public offices demonstrate desegregation efforts. I was very excited about having such a job. I had never gone to work before in an air-conditioned building wearing nice, professional clothing.

The second situation occurred because I was a product of a farming family. I applied for and received a National Defense Student Loan (NDSL); such loans were a part of President Eisenhower's plan for moving ahead of Russia in the space race after Sputnik. My father had mentioned that farmers were receiving incentives to reduce farming efforts, and I discovered what that meant. "King Cotton" was being reimagined. I received a NDSL that paid half of my college fees and a debt-free grant that paid the other half because my paperwork showed that I was a low-income minority farmer's daughter. I had no idea that the grant was a possibility when I submitted the application, but my family and I were proud to learn that half my fees were being paid.

I returned to North Texas State University in Denton, Texas, for my junior year much more confident and comfortable about leaving home and about the upcoming college coursework. There were several new dormitories on the campus, allowing more housing for African American students. I was happy to move into a new dormitory with two roommates, one of whom is still a very good friend. We were happy that although there were three students assigned to the room, we had additional space and a bathroom for our exclusive use.

I was curious as to why females of color could not enter one girls' dormitory. It was a sorority hall, and African Americans had no sororities. My curiosity led me to visit the hall one day to see what made this facility closed to me and other students of color. Upon entering the building, I found that it had a lot of beautiful attractions not usually found in student lodging: marble floors; a winding staircase with shiny banisters; and a large twinkling chandelier. I did not need those lavish quarters, but I couldn't help but wonder why that hall was not an option for my consideration. I decided that it did not matter because I was happy with the accommodations that I had.

I had enjoyable experiences at North Texas State University, now called University of North Texas (UNT), even though I was unsure of a few things. For instance, I was not always certain that the grades I received were based on performance. While I had no proof, I was certain that one instructor had given me a lower grade than I deserved. I had been warned that no minority student had ever passed his Shakespearean Literature course. I took the course anyway, and loved the literature even though there was little to no interaction during the class. I read the materials and studied them on my own. I received high marks on all assignments but never saw my final examination grade. The grade recorded was a B. Everyone who knew the situation assured me that I had earned an A. I think they were right.

During my tenure at UNT, there were signs of change: African American students organized Greek chapters; more students of color acquired university job assignments; and more students of color participated in campus organizations. A student from Paris who had taken piano lessons from the same teacher as I became one of the first black marching band members.

Instead of receiving a student teaching position in Dallas, Fort Worth, or in some remote place a world away from Denton, where UNT is located, I was assigned to student teach in an elementary school in a Denton neighborhood where many of the college professors lived. I was also chosen to drive a van provided by the university for myself and three other student teachers in that area of the city. My friends were surprised at that development, indicating that such had never happened before for an African American student.

My time at North Texas State University was very good for me, but I looked forward to graduation and moving into the world of work. Therefore, when the Reverend Martin Luther King, Jr. was assassinated on April 4, 1968, I faced a major dilemma: (1) skip classes and participate in a unity march on the day of Reverend King's funeral; or (2) attend classes as scheduled and graduate with my class the following month. Not attending classes for an unauthorized campus march would have certainly resulted in suspensions for some, if not all, students who participated. Fortunately, the university did the honorable thing and closed all classes for the event and allowed everyone related to the university to participate in a campus-wide march in honor of the well-respected civil rights leader. The weather was picture perfect, and a very large number of professors and their families, students, and others marched in the group. The Paris News had posted my picture with an article announcing that I had made the dean's list for the first semester of my senior year. I can only imagine the headline for a story one semester later about my not graduating due to a suspension from school. Whew, I breathed a sigh of relief. Everything turned out fine. I was "too close to turn around!"

A few weeks before graduation on Career Day, I was hired for a teaching position in Austin during a short interview and the ability to answer two simple questions: Who is the president of the United States? Who is the U. S. general leading the war effort in Vietnam? Having recently lost a high school classmate to the Vietnam War and with a brother headed that direction, both answers required no thought in providing the correct answers. I responded, and the interviewers seemed pleased.

The graduation ceremony for the Class of 1968 is only a blur in my mind. I heard the name of Charles Edward Greene—Mean Joe Greene--called during rehearsal. I had never met Joe Greene and only learned details about him later when he became a star football player with the Pittsburgh Steelers. I remember seeing two or three other African American students in the exercises for the Class of '68 and not much more. My family was there, and I remember leaving North Texas State University with them for the last time the night of graduation.

For my entire life, I had been comfortable with a strong support system that consisted of family—immediate and extended--friends, schools, and community. After graduation from North Texas, I considered abandoning all of that to face a different world that was totally unfamiliar to me. Giving all that up for the great unknown was a difficult decision. All through the summer, which I spent at home, I pondered over what leaving Paris meant. Maybe I was curious about an unfamiliar place, or maybe I was looking forward to being on my own for a new venture. Regardless of the reason, I leaned toward leaving for Austin. I was frightened at the thought of such a bold move. On the other hand, it was exciting to think about the wonders that awaited me in totally new surroundings and a clean slate on which to record new memories. I was headed to Austin, Texas, to begin life as a 21-year-old adult, removed from the safe, comfortable experiences I had always known.

At the end of the Summer 1968, with a bachelor's degree and $60 earned at the Paris Golf and Country Club, I went to Austin, Texas. I left Paris behind, ready to embark on a whole new journey as a self-supporting adult with a career in education.

Life on the Farm

Life of Learning

Life After the Farm

Life as an Educator

PART II

BEYOND THE FARM

MORE THAN DUTY

There is a very special person in my life;
This person listens to all my complaints and arguments.
She adjusts my tie when it isn't straight
She reminds me of the time when I'm running late.

This kind one calls my mother whenever I'm sick
And rubs my forehead until I'm calm without even a twitch
She dries my eyes whenever the tears start to flow;
She also teaches me that two plus two equals four.

She's a friend who understands my innermost thoughts
And provides the encouragement I need if I start to balk.
She picks me up whenever I feel low and down
She lights my path to success with no hint of a frown.

I can be careless, frustrating, resistant, and at times snide
But she looks deep into my soul and brings out my best side.
Day by day she toils to make me all that I can be
Ignoring all my shortcomings she works hard to teach me.

Because she never gives up on me, I know she cares
I love her because a big part of her life with me she shares.
I am the child who each and every day needs so much.
She is my teacher; she always has just the right touch.

c. j. brown

CHAPTER ELEVEN

NEW FIELDS TO FACE, NEW ROWS TO HOE

I had never been to Austin, Texas, but upon arrival there, I liked the city. The population consisted of approximately 250,000 citizens--ten times as many people as Paris had in it. Austin is the state Capital, and it is the home of the University of Texas. I was both apprehensive and happy about moving to that location. Why I chose to go where I did not know a soul and had never visited, only God knows. I certainly didn't know. I could have stayed at home and taught in Paris or in a nearby town. I was offered a contract to teach in Denton at the school where I had completed my student teaching, but I graciously declined the offer in order take the position in Austin.

The 1968 World's Fair, called Hemisfair that year, was taking place in San Antonio, so my sister, Joan, and her husband headed there for a vacation. Having to pass through Austin on their way, they dropped me off at a boarding house for young ladies located in East Austin on Twelfth Street, my new home away from home. When they drove away, I realized that I was very alone three hundred miles away from the farm and from anyone or anything that I knew.

I managed to get to school during my first few weeks as a sixth-grade school teacher, but getting there without my own car was difficult. I rode to work each morning with a co-worker who lived near my residence, but she taught only a half day leaving me to catch a taxicab home in the afternoons. That was an expense that I could not afford. Either there was no bus service near the school, or I did not understand how to manipulate the routes. At any rate, after a few weeks, my father purchased a new Camaro Rally Sports car for me. I took a bus home to Paris to pick up and drive my car back to Austin. MY VERY OWN CAR! I felt a little bad since I owned only the second new car in our family. The year before, Billy, my oldest brother, had bought the first one--also a Camaro sports vehicle.

I remained in the rooming house in order to have enough funds to make the payments on the car. Living there was strange, considering that I had nothing in common with the other young ladies or with the landlady. I moved out when the school year ended. Soon afterward, I ran into a friend who had transferred from the University of North Texas to the University of Texas. We connected and shared an apartment through the next school year. My budget was tight even with that arrangement. My car payment was exactly one-third of my monthly take home salary of $321.

I think I learned more from my students than they learned from me during my first years of teaching. I learned that all of them were different in their own ways and needed much attention. They expected me to guide them to the new learning that they were to acquire. I figured out quickly that I needed much more knowledge to meet their needs. Through self-motivation and my tendency to read a lot, I was able to acquire a better understanding of the content and the pedagogical skills necessary for teaching. The most important discovery was that daily preparation and a lot of organization were needed in order to complete all the tasks involved in being a successful teacher.

I also learned that living on my own was not as easy as I thought it would be, so I went back home to my family and the land that I had known before. I had enjoyed the Austin environment, but after two years, when I had the opportunity to teach in Paris, I did so. Jacquelyn, a younger cousin, was one of my students. Coincidentally, her mother, Aunt Gaynell, had taught me. By going home, I no longer had to worry about funds for an apartment, for food, and any other basics. No longer did I have to deal with city driving twice a day to get to and from work, and no longer did I have to cook for myself, as my mother prepared most meals—much better than those prepared by my roommate and me. Thinking back, I should have helped out more, but I lived there as an adult just as I had as a kid-- minus the field work in the hot sun. I am glad, however, that I drove with my mother in her new car to West Texas to visit Grandmother Arrie and Aunt Jim Nella and her family, a trip that Mother had wanted to make for quite some time.

By being at home I had plenty of time to study instructional practices and prepare much stronger lesson plans than I had used during my first two years of teaching. Teaching at Travis Junior High School with an understanding principal and supportive co-workers was a very productive experience. I had a chance to build skills as a teacher, and I enjoyed being with my family again. Austin, however, stayed on my mind.

I applied for and received a grant to attend the University of Texas at Austin School of Social Work (UT). I felt that I had to take advantage of that opportunity. After two years back at home, I left Paris and Northeast Texas again. I returned to Austin--this time to stay. Living at home allowed me to finish paying for my Camaro and to build a small savings account for emergencies. The social work grant program paid all tuition fees and awarded adequate funds for living expenses. Upon completing the two-year program, I was so much better prepared to face life, work, and all the accompanying complexities. In addition, I worked one year as a social worker and learned that other professions offered much higher pay than teaching. I also gained better insight into interacting with people. My interpersonal skills were enhanced through my experiences in graduate school and as a social worker in the field. That proved advantageous for me professionally and otherwise. I learned to analyze situations and give better responses to them.

Mother and Daddy, along with Uncle Kermith and Aunt June, drove to Austin for a visit during the summer between my first and second years at the UT School of Social Work. I was thrilled that they made the trip. My parents stayed with me in my small apartment, and Uncle Kermith and Aunt June stayed in a nearby hotel. Mother and Daddy could not believe that they actually spent time in an apartment. We visited several places in the city, and they thoroughly enjoyed seeing the Texas State Capitol and the rolling hills of Austin. The visit to the LBJ Presidential Library was the highlight of the trip. From their visit to Austin, they concluded that city life was safe and that I was fine living away from home in an urban environment.

It was during those two years of graduate school that I met and fell in love with the person who would become my husband, Johnny Edward Brown. Johnny was continuing on his own path to success as a coach and a teacher in Austin. We married and had three children: Berlin, Mary, and Reesha. Our wedding was held at the church, St. Mark's United Methodist Church, in which I grew up. On Sunday, April 27, 1975, the Reverend Roscoe Nunley performed our wedding ceremony. Jacquelyn, my cousin, was the organist, and Jessie, my sister-in-law, was the soloist. It was a small, but beautiful ceremony that reflected our love for each other and the humility with which we both were reared and lived by. The reception that followed was enjoyable and gave everyone from Paris and Austin a chance to meet and greet and to eat the most beautiful, delightful pineapple wedding cake ever--baked and served by none other than Aunt June.

The ceremony was held after church on Sunday so that family and friends from Austin could return to work on Monday morning. By returning to Austin that afternoon, we had one day to prepare for Johnny's knee surgery on Tuesday. Somewhere between Paris and Dallas, we were pulled over for speeding. We hoped that was not a sign of things to come. Thank God, the exact opposite was the case. The officer only issued a warning ticket. Two days later, we were in the hospital for surgery. It went well.

My job in social work ended a few months after we were married, and I returned to teaching and other educational pursuits, where I remained for a long career. My time in social work was definitely not wasted but "rounded out" the practices that I needed to become a better teacher and later a focused, goal-oriented administrator. Both my husband and I had similar paths: first as teachers; then he as counselor and I as social worker; and later as school administrators. Being in the same profession provided us a common purpose and allowed us to complement each other at home and professionally.

In meeting and marrying Johnny, I also met his family that was similar to my own. The main difference that I noticed was that I was raised in a rural environment and he was raised in the city. I had never experienced walking to school, and he had not experienced everyday rides on a school bus. His parents, Mr. Lee Boyd, Sr. and Mrs. Mary Minnie Brown, welcomed me into their fold. I thank God for that, especially since my mother passed away soon after we married. As our three children grew up, Johnny's parents and entire family were an integral part of their lives, and that was a blessing. His sisters, Joyce and Anita, and his brothers--Lee Boyd, Jr. and wife Sandra (recently deceased), Anthony and spouse, and Willie and wife Dynna—and parents spent quality time with us and our children, lending the kind of support that had a lasting impact.

Just as Johnny's family embraced me, so did my family welcome and embrace him. He became their brother, as Joan, my sister said, "We do not have any in-laws here." My father and entire family felt that Johnny was a person with integrity and were glad that I married someone of high character. They were not so sure that such a person existed in cities. Since I lived away from them, they were confident that I had made a good choice.

All three of our children grew into young adults of which we are proud. Our son, Berlin Lee, the oldest child, graduated from the University of Alabama and is employed as a computer engineer. He is named for his two grandfathers, Berlin Reese and Lee Boyd Brown. Mary Katherine, our second child, is named for her grandmothers, Katherine Reese and Mary Minnie Brown. She graduated from the same institution as her father--Texas State University--receiving a bachelor's degree in visual communications. Both Mary and her husband, Kyle Ruegg, who earned a bachelor's degree from the Kingling College of Art and Design in Florida, are employed as graphic designers. They are talented artists and are the parents of our only granddaughter, Abigail Sage. Our youngest child, Reesha Johnette, proudly wears a name formed from my maiden name, Reese, and her father's name, Johnny. She is the youngest of my parents' grandchildren. She received a bachelor's degree from the University of West Georgia and a master's degree from the University of Houston, both in communications. Reesha is a communications coordinator, and her husband, Desmond Edwards is a technology specialist who graduated from the University of Missouri.

My husband and I are great believers in reading and learning and have shared that belief with our children, encouraging them as our parents did for us. The children have seen both of us continue our training and career paths. During their young years, I acquired administration certification and worked toward a doctorate in education. Johnny earned his Master of Education degree from Texas State University and Doctor of Philosophy degree from the University of Texas at Austin. This accomplishment led to his movement into the highest leadership positions of school districts in four different states. He chronicles the successes and challenges of serving in such capacities as he tells his own story in his recent publication: <u>The Emerson Street Story: Race, Class, Quality of Life and Faith</u> (Brown, 2020).

All three of our children were born during the more than ten years that I taught in a south Austin middle school. The first home that we owned, the children's school, and my campus were all within blocks of each other in one neighborhood. The day care center that cared for the two older children after school and for the youngest throughout the day was across the street from my campus. I could look through my classroom window and see the building; that was comforting. That arrangement was difficult to give up, but I decided to spread my knowledge and experiences more widely by becoming a school administrator. By that time, Austin had grown into a much larger city than what I saw when I first went there after college. Fortunately, my next positions in Austin as assistant principal and principal were also in neighborhoods very close to home. I found that growing up as I had with a family that was purposeful in what we did with the land and life served me well as I worked with the people and challenges that I met as an administrator in Austin and in other locations.

The new paths, or new fields, of opportunities and challenges encountered in work and in everyday living added to my volume of memoirs. There were, and continues to be, endless discussions about issues of race, injustice, equality, and inequality as they relate to educating children. In my first assistant principal's job, I heard from a young special education student the best view to have regarding racial issues. In complete innocence her thoughts are captured in the following synopsis:

> *One of the young teachers had recently become a new mother. While still on maternity leave, she came back with her new infant to visit the school and her students. Hers was a biracial marriage of a couple that everyone admired. One of the teacher's students remained with her after the student body had boarded buses and gone home for the day. The young girl was clinging to her teacher and the adorable baby. The rest of us were chatting and mainly just watching the three of them*

*interact. The young student had somewhat of a puzzled look
on her face through it all, which we simply ignored as adults
often do with children.*

*The little girl finally spoke up quite emphatically, "I know.
I got it! You're white; your husband is black; and your baby
is Mexican!"*

We all looked amazed because her perception and understanding of
the race situation was that none of the color things mattered. There was
nothing there but a beautiful combination of difference and togetherness.
She spoke with conviction and without malice, prejudice, or confusing
analysis that's often wrong anyway. The young girl's underlying thought
was so pure and innocent that not one of us snickered or even smiled,
although she may have spoken in an unusual and comical manner. We all
wished that the rest of the world saw diversity with such innocence. I have
very fond memories of that moment.

Some schools had great lunches, while others had lunches that left a
lot to be desired. In an Atlanta school where I was an administrator the
cafeteria workers always prepared a salad lunch for me, something that I
would eat fast and move on to the next situation. One day I got my salad
and chose a fourth-grade table for visiting with the teacher and the students
who were seated. The teacher sat at the end of the table, and I sat in an
empty seat beside her with a student sitting directly across from me. I had
forgotten that the student was quite precocious and was being trained as
a minister. As I tore into the salad, he politely said, "Mrs. Brown, excuse
me; you forgot to say your grace. I will say it for you."

The teacher nearly lost her lunch trying to stifle laughter, and I simply
allowed him to say grace for me and thanked him for doing so. I never
forgot again to at least pause for a moment to acknowledge God before
tearing into my meal. With all the guidelines and court rulings about
prayer in school, I decided two things: (1) It is not against the rules for
children to initiate a prayer; and (2) there is no rule against having a
moment of silence at a time when a talk with the heavenly Father is
needed. The look on the student's face and the sincerity with which he

spoke remain with me. My mother often said, "Humility is a good thing and hurts no one." That was a time to be humble. I let a child lead me.

In that moment I had forgotten that modeling was one of the best ways to teach and to lead. Setting examples of excellence worked better than speeches or systems of rewards and consequences. I had trained myself to be a servant leader who did not rule by dictating. My life experiences had been positive, and I wanted my work as an educator, especially as an administrator, to reflect that side of my life. I had learned to lead by example and collaboration with all stakeholders--parents, students, and staff. That model at times took a lot of strength and a lot of strategizing. Nevertheless, based on the positive training received from my parents and from other educational leaders, that is what worked best for me as an urban educator.

CHAPTER TWELVE

URBAN EDUCATOR

The social work project that I led ended soon after Johnny and I were married, and I returned to teaching. Returning to the field of education offered me many opportunities that were exciting and uplifting and, at times, rather challenging. My first teaching assignment at that point was in the small community of Elgin, Texas, which was located about twenty-five miles east of Austin. Some of the conditions there were very familiar to me because of my days living on the farm. I could relate to the students and their circumstances. A common practice was children riding buses from and to farm homes. The high school students that I taught often faced challenges organizing work on the farm around their school schedules during the spring and fall months. I thoroughly understood when some students asked if they could reschedule exams and other class activities around "plowing the potatoes" or some other farm chore. There were two big differences from what I experienced as a child: White students, black students, and Hispanic students attended school together, whereas only black students attended school with me while I was growing up, and the high school had a football team that the entire town was proud of because they were a winning team, whereas, Powderly High School was not large enough to have a football team.

The experience in Elgin was a definite reminder of my old school days, and I enjoyed working there. However, once we bought our first home in South Austin far from Elgin, I began teaching in Austin again. I taught English and reading at Roy Bedichek Middle School near my residence for ten and one-half years. I was recognized in various ways while working at that campus: Teacher of the Year; invitations to serve on school district planning committees; and chairperson of a campus-wide initiative to improve academic achievement. I joined the Delta Kappa Gamma Society International--a sorority for women educators--and later became president of the chapter due to my success while at that campus. The principals and staff there indeed made work seem like family and home. Working within blocks of our children's schools was an added bonus.

I had many rewarding experiences while teaching at Bedichek, including assisting the campus in transitioning from a junior high school with grades seven-eight to a middle school with grades six-eight. As a teacher, I had taught at the elementary, middle, and high school levels. The students at Bedichek Middle School were generally cooperative and well behaved; however, during one of my years there, I had some very challenging students. I had two difficult groups, one more so than the other. All members of the more difficult group had some kind of issue ranging from struggling learner status to gang affiliation. They showed resistance to any attempts at improving their reading abilities. I decided that I would teach them no matter what. I needed new, relevant materials, which the principal allowed me to buy with school funds even though he had declared that there could be no more purchases of instructional materials during that year. I set up a circular seating arrangement because turning my back on the students was not a good idea. We started reading materials together with a lot of discussion and dialogue and, at times, role playing. Our written work was done as a team. Positive changes started to occur. As a group, we became close, and learning was the new focus. By Christmas we were studying The Outsiders by S. E. Hinton. We sat on the floor and watched the movie made from the novel on the last day of school before the winter holidays. I knew that something unusual was going on with them as the movie played. However, I made no move to investigate because by that time we had learned to trust each other, and I did not feel threatened by their secret activity. After the movie ended, the class made a presentation to me of gifts and a homemade greeting card containing notes from each class member. I was very touched when I realized what they had been up to. What made the gifts so special is that some of them were personal treasures--before regifting was a trend. I was speechless and had great difficulty holding back tears because they let me know that I had touched them in a significant way. That group made stronger my conviction that students from diverse backgrounds can be reached and experience success when they know that adults care about them.

The first administrative position that I assumed was migrant consultant with Ms. Lee Laws as director of governmental programs. Lee was an extremely knowledgeable and well-respected administrator. Coincidentally, she was the person, along with my husband, who had earlier encouraged me to go back to graduate school to add educational administration certification to my master's degree. I am thankful for the guidance that she provided. She shared a wealth of knowledge that I used throughout the remainder of my career. I was fortunate and blessed to work with other great leaders in all of the positions that I held since that time: principals, directors, and superintendents. Each position better prepared me for the next one. The positions called for hard work, which I was accustomed to from living on the farm. I appreciated working in the same line of employment as my husband. Our own children were school aged by that time; therefore, my home life and my work life were seamless experiences.

All of my administration work took place in urban settings composed of diverse populations. While large cities may have diverse populations, I found that providing high quality educational experiences and genuine concern for children produced successful outcomes regardless of students' backgrounds, race, or other circumstances. When my husband obtained a position as deputy superintendent in Cleveland, Ohio, I became a principal there. Cleveland is a large urban center. A few things stood out in taking that assignment: I had no experience as a principal even though I had been an assistant principal and a central office administrator; I had never worked with unions that had real negotiating power; and I had not lived in a northern location since my entire existence had been in Texas.

During my first visit to Miles Elementary School, I saw a building that had been erected at least seventy-five years earlier. The building was very sturdy, which was typical of structures in the North, and not much about it had changed. The original wood floors were in place, and the desks were similar to the ones that I remembered from my old school days. The preparation for Open House "broke the ice" with the staff members. As we discussed proceedings for that upcoming event, I suggested that perhaps we should post student work, possibly with common themes, as a whole school or as grade level teams. The staff members started talking all at once about what they could do to make their classrooms reflect their instruction. When I expressed that I was glad to see such enthusiasm about displaying work and wondered what caused the change, they responded, "We thought we couldn't put anything up and always wondered why not."

I explained, "I do not know what gave you that idea, but please feel free to display work and create the learning environment that best fits your instruction." I have no idea where that thought had come from, but I was glad to see the building come alive with student work and other artifacts that reflected learning. Why the teachers and staff members had thought otherwise was unimportant.

As part of the district's school reform initiative for academic improvement, my campus focused on becoming an Afrocentric school with a curriculum that combined an Afrocentric educational approach with the usual academic learning. The teachers and parents chose this model of academic reform because they believed it would be good for the population of students, which was 70% African American and 30% Anglo, or white. Both groups could learn about the African past and apply that information to the students' current real-life circumstances. The model included motivational components and viable curriculum and instruction practices that focused on improving academic performance. One of the designers of the model, Molefi Asante from Temple University, was often present to conduct workshop sessions, which was energizing for all the stakeholders. I was recruited back to Austin to assume a principal's position for the next school year, so I did not see the full implementation of the school reform model nor the test results for comparison. I am confident that my successor led the initiative effectively.

A large United States Steel (USS) plant had operated not very far from the school several years beforehand. However, when I arrived in Cleveland, blocks of emptiness were the only indicators of incomes and comfortable life styles long since gone. The Miles Elementary School neighborhood reflected the loss of income and middle-class life styles caused by the closure of that USS plant.

The first task for me each morning was to survey the building and surroundings to assess the condition of the environment. Ice presented a constant challenge. The below freezing temperatures kept the streets and parking lot iced over, making accidents a common occurrence. De-icing was almost a daily need for some months, and any missed spots could result in a major problem. In only one day a teacher broke a leg while getting into her car ready to drive to work, and a student fell on the school parking lot, breaking both legs.

Our daughter, Mary, slipped on the playground at her school one day and sprained an ankle, no breaks. I picked her up and took her to the emergency room at the Cleveland Clinic, one of the most well-known medical facilities of the world. Cleveland was like that--some situations were very lacking while others were well known for high quality service. For example, the Cleveland orchestra had a world-famous conductor and remains one of the "Big Five" orchestras in the United States. On Saturday afternoons, I enjoyed watching the peaceful snow and drinking hot chocolate while all three of our children took lessons at The Cleveland Institute of Music, a highly acclaimed music center, connected with Case Western Reserve University.

Speaking of ice and snow, having lived my whole life in Texas, I had no idea what real cold was or what real winter wear was. The lowest temperature in Paris that I can remember was 15 degrees Fahrenheit a few mornings each year. The lowest temperature that I remember for Cleveland was 20 degrees below zero--fifty-two degrees below freezing; add the wind chill factor, and the temperature felt like 40-45 degrees below zero. Our entire family had to buy new clothing to match the freezing temperatures that remained throughout the winter months. We learned a lasting lesson about cold weather while attending the state championship game for our son's high school varsity football team. We thought we were dressed for cold, but we soon realized that we had no clue. The other families had foot warmers, seat warmers, and other heat paraphernalia unfamiliar to us. We wore the big coats, gloves, and other winter attire that we had brought from Texas, but our clothes did not stand a chance against the brutal cold that we faced in the stands of that stadium. When Reesha, our youngest child, announced that her fingers had fallen off, we gave up and headed to the car. Our son, Berlin, was not playing anyway because he had broken his wrist during an earlier practice session. The team won the championship game as they had done for five of the last six years. The school had an exceptional academic program and the same for football.

It was very cold outside, but the insides were hotter than the fields of Northeast Texas. The staff members explained that in Cleveland you must wear layers--thick layers--that can be peeled off once inside since "nature keeps it very cold outside, and the old coal-fueled furnaces and thick insulation materials keep it very hot inside." I learned to listen to the teachers and staff about the climate and about a lot of other things. However, they had not prepared me for the kind of incident that occurred one sunny afternoon as we dismissed our students.

The buses started to pull out of the parking lot that was also our playground, as a car came careening down the street with another car directly behind on its tail. A young woman was driving a fancy sports car. A male driver of a second fancy sports car braked quickly, ran to the first car, snatched the keys from the ignition, beat out the back window with his fists, ran back to get into his car and just as quickly backed it down the street at breakneck speed. The lady driver and the buses waiting to pull into the street where her car sat were stuck. Some windows of the first bus were open, and a few children cried as the glass flew inside. I was the only person horrified enough and foolish enough to try to stop the gentleman-- term used lightly--from completing his task. The teachers and other adults shook their heads and asked, "Do you really think you should try to stop a man like that?" I did not reply, as the answer was obvious.

Regardless of such incidents, I always felt comfortable at Miles Elementary School, even late in the evenings because the parents were committed to watching out for me and always said, "Don't worry. We never turn our porch lights off until you are gone."

With the help of the parents and community, we had excellent programs, and learning improved. One culminating learning event that demonstrated our growth was part of a district bond campaign. The teachers and parents organized a parade, complete with guest speakers, cars, treats, adults on every corner, and any other needed supports. Everyone enjoyed the event, indicating that this was the first time in years that the students and teachers had come out into the community.

I developed a remarkable rapport with the students, staff, parents, and entire community in a short time. I left the school after one year feeling that I had made a difference there with my East Texas accent, country logic, and any ideas that I could create to make up for my lack of experience. I also left the school with a new interior paint job, compliments of a collaborative effort with the Cleveland Police Department.

There were similar circumstances in other locations where I worked. However, I was better prepared for meeting new challenges because I had more experience and I had access to more resources. I was recruited back to Austin to become principal of a school where the teachers were dedicated, and the families knew each other and supported the school well. The campus was near my home in a community of families who had low to mid-incomes and enjoyed a mixture of three ethnic groups: black, white, and Hispanic. With great teamwork the first year we moved the mathematics scores from 29% to 66% of the students mastering the state test. My supervisor read the data wrong and sent me a correspondence asking about the big drop. I sent a correspondence back indicating that he had read the data backwards and that our results were the opposite of what he thought. We both were happy about that.

I left that position during the third year in order to assume an administrative post at the education service center in Dallas. My husband, Johnny, served as superintendent in a school district in metro-Dallas at that time. Following our time in the Dallas area, my family moved to Birmingham, Alabama, and I became the Director of Curriculum for the Fairfield City Schools in Alabama.

The position as Director of Curriculum in Fairfield was my second central office experience. Working directly with Dr. Yvette Richardson, superintendent, with the Director of Federal Programs, and others was exhilarating. I "wore many hats." We all worked hard, but the results were worth the effort. Most of the 2,700 students were African American with mixed incomes. In one year, in collaboration with the Alabama State Department of Education, we flipped the test results from all schools but one scoring in the alert (low performing) status to all schools but one scoring in the clear, acceptable, status. Coincidentally, like Cleveland, Fairfield had been home to a large United States Steel plant that was now only a reminder of resources that no longer existed.

I was involved with curriculum projects at the Alabama State Department of Education on more than one instance, and that was advantageous for my educational growth. As soon as I arrived in Birmingham, I was asked to go to Mobile, Alabama, to attend the first meeting for a curriculum alignment project led by the state curriculum team. I thought, "No problem; I will drive down and back." I did not realize that the drive would be as long and lonely as it turned out to be. The pine trees on both sides of the highway were thick and taller than any that I had ever seen, including those near my home in East Texas. I soon grew weary after seeing nothing else for hours. Finally, I arrived at the convention center in Mobile and attended the meeting, only to turn around and make the long, lonely trip back to Birmingham. After about an hour and a half, I was too tired to continue driving and saw a sign for the city of Monroeville and decided to pull over and to take a nap in the car at a hotel on the access road. I later learned that I was near the hometown of Truman Capote and Harper Lee, authors of <u>In Cold Blood</u> and <u>To Kill a Mockingbird</u>, respectively. Monroeville is also the location of the <u>Just Mercy</u> saga in which a young lawyer was determined to obtain freedom for a falsely accused death row inmate. The late 1980s true story is reflected in both a book and a 2019 award-winning movie. I promised myself that I would do some research on where I was going before making another such trip.

The trip to Mobile was the first meeting to launch a major collaborative to support a new state graduation examination. The Alabama State Department of Education leaders were concerned that implementing a new, more rigorous assessment would show a decrease in student achievement and wanted to avoid such an outcome. Therefore, they put together a team of fifty teachers and directors of curriculum to devise lessons and activities to address every standard that would be assessed in each subject area. One teacher from the district and I made several trips to the State Department in Montgomery to work on the project. It was a daunting, but worthy, task. After creating the teaching materials, we conducted workshops throughout the state for administrators and teachers about the ways in which to use the documents. The project was successful for the schools of the state, including the high school in Fairfield.

I participated in several rewarding activities while working in Fairfield in collaboration with institutions of higher learning, with the Alabama State Department of Education, and with other school systems. The work in Fairfield was demanding but fulfilling because I was able to connect in some way to everyone there from the students and their families to the school board.

Later, I moved with my family to Dekalb County, Georgia, and I assumed a position in Atlanta located in an area similar to the one in Cleveland. The two schools were somewhat alike demographically, but resources were more accessible in Atlanta. The learning environment was engaging and fostered increases in achievement. We became a turn around campus, meeting federal and state standards, during my first year there and continued to grow from that point. An integral part of the instruction was the implementation of three major reform initiatives--first reading, second mathematics, and thirdly discipline and management. Teamwork was very strong as we worked closely with the students and their families to implement the new reform models. Implementation of the reform models was rewarding because the design and the expected outcomes were clear, easily followed and easily measured. I have very fond memories of my regular trips into the neighborhoods, often after school hours when families were outside. Parents sometimes said, "Excuse me, Ms. Brown," and went on with their activities, using colorful language and interesting topics. I was never surprised at anything during my visits. While the language might have been "rich," I always felt part of the community. Home visits helped me better understand the kinds of considerations necessary for success in the environment in which I worked.

My next and last job assignment was in Port Arthur, Texas, where my husband was the superintendent of the school district. As English Language Arts Curriculum Supervisor, I appreciated the opportunity to work with students and teachers to improve reading and writing. One highlight of my time there was coordinating the district's Annual Academic Bowl, a fun quiz bowl event focused on academic competition. The entire school system participated. Every campus except those with only primary grades had a team of contestants, and every department in the district had a role to play in the implementation of the event, from bus drivers to administrators. The curriculum and instruction department, along with the technology and other district teams, worked hard to make this event an example of how urban education can work well for children when the resources are put in place. School Board members, parents, and other community representatives attended the event to watch the teams compete to demonstrate knowledge of content from every subject area. This event was a shining example of academic excellence where an entire community supported learning in an exciting, productive manner.

There are times in education when school leaders have to address social and personal concerns of a dire nature: clothing, food, or money; answering the needs of students with dyslexia, dysgraphia, autism, bi-polar disorder, and other learning conditions; homelessness; abuse; and other challenges. Oftentimes such concerns are not mentioned when various aspects of education, such as test results, are discussed. There are times when mere survival, take priority, and high-stakes tests are not the only means for determining preparedness for life after secondary school. While growing up in a rural area of Northeast Texas, some students were less capable academically but were loved and made to feel important for other accomplishments. Most of those students became productive members of society leading comfortable lives as contributing members of society.

High stakes testing has its place in education to hold educators--and students--accountable for what they should learn and to ensure quality educations for all. However, the surrounding conditions, the differing abilities and talents of each student, the resources provided, and how the resources are allocated and utilized make it difficult to determine what students have actually achieved. Add competition for resources, labeling of children, teacher preparation, natural disasters, pandemics and other unexpected disruptions, and the attempt to accurately measure what students really know becomes a colossal task.

I attended a technology conference at the Georgia Dome of Atlanta during my tenure as the Director of Curriculum in Fairfield, Alabama. The high school principal and I, accompanied by our youngest daughter, Reesha, attended the conference where many technological advancements for use in 21st century learning were demonstrated. The high point of the conference for me was hearing The Honorable Richard Riley, Secretary of Education, deliver the keynote address. I have a problem being prompt, so arriving at a 7:45 a.m. opening assembly was challenging, but I got there. Along with thousands of other educators, I listened to the secretary's inspiring speech. In his comfortable style and voice, he declared with conviction, "High stakes testing was designed to increase student achievement and was intended to help improve instruction and learning. It was never meant to traumatize teachers and students." The applause was thunderous, and lasted for quite some time.

Trying to determine what students know is a monumental undertaking. Gathering such information for reading is an even greater task. Since there are such great concerns about literacy instruction and assessment, more attention should be directed to that component of the curriculum. Taking different approaches to assessment and instruction in literacy might provide more satisfactory answers to the numerous questions about reading performance.

CHAPTER THIRTEEN

THE THREE RS - READ, READ, READ

Reading is a major concern in education, possibly more so in urban settings simply because there are so many more students involved for consideration. Of course, with greater numbers in the student population, the more difference in backgrounds. Each year when test results are released, the question is commonly asked, "Why can't they read?" The question comes from many directions and sources, and the answers come from even more directions and sources: school leaders; teachers--especially those who teach in other content areas; parents; community leaders; business experts; college and university professors; and others. A few of the explanations provided are as follows:

- Their parents don't read and don't read to them.
- They don't know the basics.
- They don't like to read.
- They don't have books at home.
- They lack background knowledge, no exposure.
- Teachers don't know how to teach phonics.
- They are not taught in small groups.
- They have so many deficiencies.
- They can't write either.

Most responders have never met the children and do not know them personally. Therefore, they cannot really discern what the real challenges are. Probably all of the above answers apply in some sense, but could be changed with a paradigm shift that includes looking at the situation differently. Posing a different set of questions might better address the concerns about reading proficiency. Consider the following:

1. Are the current high stakes tests the best measures of reading proficiency?
2. Can the tests be designed differently to better reflect the instructional practices experienced and the skills learned by the students?
3. Can tests include more content that mirrors the real-life experiences of all students, not just those students in groups familiar to the crafters of the tests?

Since reading is the "gateway" subject for all other content areas, we might benefit from looking at the assessments in that subject differently. The high stakes test outcomes could be used to gather baseline data about a child's reading proficiency. If the test results indicate low performance, additional assessment measures designed to determine underlying causes of deficiencies should be administered so that instruction can be tailored to address specific identified needs. Rather than labeling children beginning in third grade—eight years old--as non-readers, once test results are received, additional information can be gathered and compiled to design more explicit reading instruction. Teacher observations, parent conferences, fluency checks, running records, and other assessments can provide comprehensive profiles to address deficits in preparation for a better result on the future high-stakes tests. Such a model indicates, as the Honorable Richard Riley suggested, that ongoing assessments should be utilized to make informed decisions about improving achievement instead of administering the same test year after year to get the same, or worse, results. Alfred Tatum, offered the following: "Identifying students' literacy-related strengths and weakness requires an assessment approach that is ongoing, involves both formal and informal techniques, and extends across several areas of reading. The teacher's assessment practices have to be wide enough and frequent enough in order to provide effective, responsive instruction." (Tatum, 2005, p. 124).

My husband, Johnny, and I spent an inspiring evening having dinner with Dr. Tatum as one activity of a state conference. He shared with those of us fortunate enough to sit at his table his successes in getting troubled males in the Chicago area to read and to appreciate literature. The dialogue with Dr. Tatum was time well spent with good food and unbelievable knowledge of practices that actually work in teaching reading.

Providing greater clarity, or specificity, of the curriculum standards would be a major step in adjusting the instruction-assessment continuum. Current reading standards include a strong emphasis on inferential and analytical thinking. In order to master these skills, students are taught to "make educated guesses" and to "read between the lines," which are idiomatic statements that simply add to the confusion, particularly for first-time English learners. Mike Schmoker suggests that the lack of specificity in English language arts standards is a problem, and he stated, "Language arts, more than any other discipline, has lost its way. It is in desperate need of clarity. To that end, we need to simplify and reconceive English language arts standards. Without meaning to, state standards and assessments have had a uniquely destructive effect here. As currently conceived, they have corrupted language education and its essential mission: to ensure that students can read, write, and speak effectively in and out of school" (Schmoker, 2011, p. 93).

No one expects a comfortable living room environment while testing, but on test administration days students are herded into tense settings to sit for many hours, four to five hours in some cases, to read and answer complex questions to five or more selections up to three pages in length in one sitting. This structure is in sharp contrast to the regular classroom design and real life circumstances where scholars often study and analyze as teams with a teacher facilitating one selection for up to five or more days. Fewer, and perhaps shorter, passages to master might give a better measurement of a student's ability to read and analyze selections. Are we measuring ability or endurance?

Rigor is expected, but confusing, ambiguous questions only frustrate struggling learners in a tense testing environment. A better balance of abstract questions with concrete questions would allow readers whose higher order thinking skills are still developing more success on high stakes tests. Both developing and advanced readers could benefit from such a consideration.

Higher proficiency in reading and all subjects will result by providing greater clarity of what should be learned, consistent instructional practices designed to master the standards, administration of tests that reflect the instruction, and a sense of urgency in ensuring that all children learn at their optimum levels. Approaching the situation from a problem-solving perspective may yield different outcomes and possibly reveal that many of the children thought to be non-readers can indeed read. Instead of asking why can't they read, we might focus on what really works to increase reading achievement.

I always enjoyed reading and writing; therefore, the fact that I followed a literacy path should be no surprise. Since I always liked to read, the part of my work that was most gratifying for me was training students and teachers in strategies for increasing reading proficiency. I usually worked with teachers, but I always found time to interact with students. My employment as English Language Arts Curriculum Supervisor in Port Arthur, the last position that I held, allowed me to focus solely on literacy. Working with reading, writing, and books was fun work, which led to my remaining in that position at least half a decade longer than I originally intended. The first task that I took on upon working in that capacity was to get books into classrooms. I worked with administrators to get an average of 125 books into every elementary and secondary language arts classroom in the school district. In addition, we designed a reading center for several fifth-grade students from designated schools to experience extended reading training and many, many books. The center's library had unlimited books for students in the program to access without any restriction. Wide exposure to books is one of the first steps to increasing reading proficiency.

In designing training sessions for either teachers or students, developing a rapport with the audience is the first consideration. By the time I assumed the position as English Language Arts Curriculum Supervisor in Port Arthur, our own children were grown and working on their own, but they were good resources when I was stomped and needed a young person's perspective on any aspect of an upcoming presentation.

They helped with ideas on the latest trends in music, fashion, and other trending youth and young adult issues. Mary's paintings were often included in presentations for writing topics and discussions of inferences to be made regarding her intent and how she built the illustrations for her own purposes. Her portrait of our dog, Coach, generated a lot of interest. Reesha's "infinite wisdom" about growing up and about life in general made interesting discussion topics. I sometimes shared entertaining stories about her--some real and some not so real. I always told her, "If someone comes up to you to share an entertaining tale about you, just nod and say nothing." In addition, her own news articles came in very handy as examples of good writing when she lived with us and worked for the Port Arthur News. I called on our son, Berlin, when I was stuck on trying to connect mathematics to reading and writing. I always let the audience know which child I was referencing; they found that either amazing or amazingly comical. Connecting to teachers, certainly to students, is the first step toward building a successful reading program. Half the battle to improving reading proficiency is having an atmosphere that makes reading comfortable and inviting.

One strategy that works well with both students and teachers is a group chant or a short poem, such as the following:

I AM AN AUTHOR

Writing is thinking
I am a thinker
Therefore, I am an author.
All it takes is a topic
Add supporting details
Organize my thoughts.
Begin with some bing
End with a bang
There you have it
I'm all done—
Know what?
I think I'll do another one.

This poem works well for short breaks when developing compositions, which can sometimes be a long, tedious process. Starting a reading unit or reminding the audience, especially students, of the unit's purpose is much easier with a simple chant such as this one:

I SEE IT

I SAY IT

I THINK IT

I KNOW IT!

Those few words translate into an effective reading formula: look at the print and all visuals; read the selection carefully; analyze the author's meaning; and understand what was read. Videos on almost every topic imaginable are available and serve as great supports for engaging students in "the work." Often students have little or no background knowledge about a reading topic. With chants, videos, short research projects--time to pull out cell phones, which they all have--students start to connect to the content. Use of technology is motivational for students, and *wanting* to read is vastly important to the whole process.

Four male high school students attended a conference workshop session that I was conducting for several teachers and administrators. In an assembly earlier that morning the four students had articulated well their views of teaching and learning. One of the students, an obviously bright young man, stated that he did not like to read. I knew that he was challenging me to explain how I would motivate young people to read when they were choosing not to. I was a little caught off guard and needed a moment to prepare a response, so I said, "Hold that thought."

He replied, "Okay."

After sharing a few ideas about the importance of reading, I spoke about different ways and different reasons to read. I then abruptly asked, "What is the tallest building in the world?" After a few awkward moments of silence, one of the students pulled out his cell phone to find the answer. The other students followed suit. The adults saw the students researching the answer and pulled out their various devices. Everybody in the room began reading about the tallest buildings in the world and engaged in conversations about why it is not clear which building is really tallest because multiple countries are competing for that title with architectural wonders that are reaching unimaginable heights—pun intended. When I had to stop the conversations due to time constraints, the student who had asked the question laughed and said, "You tricked me. By asking a question that you knew no one had an answer to, we had to figure it out. We read, discussed, and learned more than was asked for."

It was apparent that the exchanges generated by the question were far more important than the answer. I thanked him for asking the question and moved on. I had gotten the idea a couple of years before from a High School That Works conference. When students want to read, they read. The more they read, the better readers they become. Phyllis C. Hunter commented, "I hear it all the time: kids these days don't like to read; kids these days are lazy; kids these days spend all their time playing video games. Well, guess what? It's not true. Kids these days are reading and writing as much as ever…and in some cases, more than ever. It all depends on a simple question: What do we consider reading?" (Hunter, 2012, p. 15).

Working together is a great way for students to help each other learn. Group projects are effective mechanisms for training students to work in teams to accomplish school tasks and for being successful once they enter the world of work. Reading and writing are communication tools; therefore, classrooms should promote communicating and sharing opportunities. Students learn more when they pool their individual strengths. "The whole is greater than the sum of its parts," said Aristotle.

Teamwork is a soft skill in which employers tell educators that students are the least proficient. Company leaders often say, "You send them to us without their knowing how to work together in teams." Leading schools through implementation of reform models, all of which included cooperative learning, has made me a firm believer in the value of having students accomplish tasks together. Teamwork removes much of the threat involved in having to master difficult print material. Students support each other while searching to understand printed materials, freeing up their minds to delve deeper into the rigor that is a part of their learning. Children enjoy reading and analyzing together. Even though it takes planning and organization, the final outcome is worth it. Class activities must contain individual work, too. There has to be a balance of both group and individual activities because life is a combination of both types of interactions. With new environmental restrictions caused by a devastating pandemic, creativity is needed in the implementation of such work. Just as music directors can train choirs and bands to sing and play together online from different locations, teachers and parents can devise strategies to facilitate students' working together on reading tasks, regardless of the locations and circumstances. Under both normal and unusual circumstances there are strategies that support team interactions, such as the following:

> **Think-Pair-Share.** Think-Pair-Share is a collaborative strategy in which a class of students are given a question to answer. They think about the question for a short, specified amount of time, one minute or so. Next, two assigned partners pair up to share and compare their thoughts about applicable answers. Time may allow sharing out to an entire class.

> **Think-Turn-Talk.** This strategy is very similar to Think-Pair-Share. After receiving a prompt, a student thinks about a proper response and then turns to a "shoulder partner" sitting beside him or her. A student may be asked to share with an "Eyeball partner" sitting across the table or with a "clock partner" located in another part of the room. Clock partners are established earlier in the instructional process.

> **Sticky Notes.** Post-it Notes are used by individuals or groups of students to respond to a prompt and display the responses on large sheets of paper attached to the walls of the room. **Gallery Walks** take place afterwards so that individuals or teams can move about the room and share feedback for the responses exhibited. Feedback can be provided in short comments or through the use of symbols, such as + *for excellent, -for revisit, or ? for unclear.*

I often end sessions with the Power of Three--a random number that I happen to like--when there isn't enough time for everyone to share. At least three groups conclude a class session by briefly explaining their work over an assigned activity to the entire class. The wrap-up and reflection time brings everyone together for a last-minute look at the learning that took place and sets the stage for the next day's work. For a writing lesson, ending reflections might be rendered in terms of thoughts about the assignment, or three students might share a part or all of their compositions. The sharing of responses to reading, or other literacy activities, incorporate socialization skills and expands the amount of learning that each individual attains.

No matter what content students are attempting to master, the work should be worthwhile and engaging. Active involvement rather than passive listening leads to greater comprehension of text. Once specific goals are established for working to understand a selection, reading charts and diagrams such as those included in The Brown Book Bag (appendix) help to focus students' attention on various components or elements needed to analyze--dissect and pick apart--passages. When students engage in hands-on activities in reading, as in other subjects, in-depth, higher-order thinking occurs, and their chances for test mastery and for sustained learning are much greater. Students can work together in teams, relaxing in positions on the floor, around tables, in hallways, or in other less traditional spots to complete their work when using visuals. Crayons and markers to use with large pieces of paper, such as newsprint or butcher paper, boxes, and other containers are great for creating different versions of teacher-made visuals. Such activities are effective for school or home use. Teachers and parents should be careful and creative with cooperative groupings during a health crisis, like the COVID-19 pandemic. They can use individual copies rather than a large, single copy to work from and can interact inside a classroom or from afar using computers and other digital devices for conversation. Children have fun, when they are actively involved in hands-on learning activities. After they participate in learning games, creating visuals, and sharing their results with classmates, they often leave class commenting, "We didn't work today; we just had fun." They don't realize they actually connected to reading materials in a meaningful way, minus the tension and displeasure often associated with the instruction. Reading interest, and subsequently reading proficiency, increases when reading is a joy, not a chore and a bore.

Some adults are hesitant to have students, especially older ones, actively interacting with each other related to reading assignments. Adults fear that students will take advantage of such work to get off task or that hands-on work is reserved for "the little ones." Regardless of age, students enjoy work that involves more than reading and answering questions. Engaging activities help to master skills needed for understanding what is read.

Students should learn and practice certain comprehension skills and strategies while reading. Some of the common skills to master are described below.

Author's Craft. Author's craft refers to the style and methods used by the writer to create meaning in a selection. Understanding how author's construct their selections aids comprehension. To create effect, some authors use punctuation marks: commas, exclamations, question marks, periods, hyphens, and other physical symbols. Other writers use repetition, sound words like *hiss-ss*, comparisons, contrasts, and even humor to capture a reader's attention. An example of repetition and punctuation used for emphasis follows: Wow! jumping and running are fun activities; jumping and running are good exercise experiences; jumping and running are good for the mind--and the body. Do you like these activities?

Cause and Effect. This skill includes looking at certain details and determining how one impacts the other. Example: A bump developed on the child's forehead after a large box fell from a high shelf onto her head. Cause (why)--a large box fell on her; effect (what)--a bump developed. Students must visualize which event occurred first as the cause and which event happened secondly as a result of the first occurrence.

Compare-Contrast. Comparing and contrasting involves reading all or part of a selection and deciding what is alike and what is different. Students can be guided to compare and contrast one product to another product, one occurrence to another occurrence, one character with another character, or one entire selection to another selection. An example: Golf and bowling are alike and different in several ways. Golf is played outside on a golf course, while bowling is played inside in a bowling alley. Golf is played with a club and a very small ball, while bowling is played with a large, heavy ball and pins. Both sports require special shoes. (See appendix.)

Inference. A large percentage of the questions found on today's high stakes tests are inferential. Very few questions ask for literal responses that are easily detected by looking back at the selections. Making inferences requires mixing clues from the passages with prior knowledge and personal experiences to make good judgment about what is happening in a selection. In The Boy Who Harnessed the Wind the narrator stated, "...secondary school was a privilege and an honor." The speaker left the reader to infer that in his country attending school after the elementary level required meeting certain competitive conditions or payment and only select ones moved on to that level (Kamkwamba and Mealer, 2015. p. 106).

Point-of-View. Point of view is very important. Students should know who is speaking in a story or passage. Identifying the speaker helps with making inferences because the reader can have mental conversations with that person. Students look at a selection and decide whether a character or the author is "talking" and quickly determine first person, second person, or third person. The thinking, however, should go much deeper to analyze how the point of view affects what is happening in the selection. For example, in a composition about the importance of football in a young person's life, the ideas and opinions will vary based on who is speaking. The coach has one perspective about the sport versus the grandmother who winces at every play that includes her grandson. The grandson's view is unlike that of either adult.

Theme. It is important that readers recognize theme, or the main idea, presented in any selection. Theme is a life lesson that has three characteristics: (1) It is an overarching principle about life for everyone, not just the characters in the text; (2) It is a complete thought, not a one-word topic; and (3) It is the overall thought that flows throughout the entire selection--the big picture--not an isolated detail. Here are some examples: Money can't buy happiness. You can't judge a book by its cover. Honesty is the best policy. Love conquers all.

Students will be better prepared to face challenging literacy tests If they learn to think deeply about what they read. Visuals are representations of print material that help to clarify students' thinking. Examples of visuals such as those included in the appendix can be used in a classroom or at home for "mind mapping" or thinking about reading.

Independent reading is one of the greatest ways to increase test results. There is a direct correlation between the amount of independent reading and high stakes test results. Exposure to words and language in many formats affects reading results. Fisher and Frey (2018) researched the work of other experts to share the following:

> *Stanovich (1986) examined the relationship between students' volume of outside reading and their ability to read. This study confirmed what many teachers had always known—the more reading students do, the better their reading becomes. A related study compared students' standardized test scores in reading and the amount of outside reading they did. As in the earlier study, the results indicated that there was a strong correlation between reading volume and achievement (Anderson, et al. 1988).*

A table that accompanies the research shows that when students read 9.6 minutes per day, they scored at the 70th percentile on high stakes tests.

If they read 65 minutes per day--just a little more than an hour--they scored at the 98th percentile (Fisher and Frey, 2018, p. 113).

Building environments that foster positive connections to literature improve reading proficiency because children read more when they enjoy reading. Fisher and Frey (2018) share more research findings on the subject: "A large-scale study based on national testing results suggested that students who had positive attitudes toward reading (*described as engaged readers*) outperformed older, disengaged readers (Campbell, et al. 1997). An analysis of fourth graders' results on the same test revealed that engaged readers from low-income backgrounds outperformed disengaged readers from higher socioeconomic backgrounds" (Guthrie, et al.).

While working as a curriculum supervisor in Port Arthur, we joined other schools and districts in the country in the Read Across America celebrations of Dr. Seuss's birthday. For one week leading up to Dr. Seuss's birthday all sixteen campuses in the district conducted various activities to foster interest in reading: visitors and staff members from throughout the community read to students; students and teachers participated in character parades; door decorating contests occurred; campus-wide literacy fairs included carnival games and other fun activities for children and adults; and the Dr. Seuss theme was included in the regular instruction of all content areas. Rhonda Calcote added a district-wide Literacy Night to the Dr. Seuss activities when she joined the team of curriculum supervisors. In this event, students were recognized with awards and certificates for accruing exceptional numbers of points based on comprehension tests about books. In addition, student representatives from each campus presented poems, plays, and other literacy performances, including lyrical dances. The entire community was involved in a week of celebrating books.

"Out-of-the-box" thinking is required to actively engage all students, including English Learners (ELs) and others, in productive, interesting literacy exchanges. Marley Dias, a phenomenal young lady, took an "out-of-the-box" approach to one reading issue--relevancy. I had the opportunity of meeting and hearing Marley speak at the 2018 International Literacy Association conference when she was only thirteen years old. She shared that she liked to read but realized that the books on her reading lists would not appeal to other African American students because they did not include African American characters or topics to which African

American children could relate. She was especially concerned about black girls not seeing black female role models in the books on the assigned reading lists. Readers need to see characters in books who look like them. Marley decided to begin a campaign to gather books about black people to distribute to black children. She created a hashtag, #100BlackGirlBooks, and used social media to publicize her initiative. Within a few months, she collected more than 1000 books, which she and her parents donated to a school and a library in Jamaica. The project quickly increased to 10,000 books (Dias, 2018).

In thinking about her school's reading lists--made up of classics--she wondered why so many accomplished black authors were omitted, including Newbery Medal winners. She raised the question thusly: "Roll of Thunder, Hear My Cry by Mildred D. Taylor won the 1977 Newbery Medal. It had been around a long time like those other books. Why wasn't it considered a classic?" (Dias, 2018, p. 25). Marley explained the importance of gaining a Newbery Award by saying, "It's like winning an Oscar for your book; if you win it, you are basically officially one of the best authors on the planet" (Dias, 2018, p. 23). Marley's initiative put books of interest into the hands of thousands of students. A girl of thirteen looked at the relevancy problem and offered a logical, effective solution.

It is often assumed that inordinate amounts of time and effort are needed to create effective literacy programs, but often the answers are quite simple. For instance, adults and children reading together provides enjoyable exchanges and contribute immensely to growth in proficiency and to adult-child bonding. I love reading aloud to children and adults of all ages. With discussion and dialogue, not interrogation, of such materials, students develop interest and ask for more because the books contain content related to them and their real-life circumstances. Popular book titles to include are Maniac Magee by Jerry Spinelli, Under the Mesquite by Guadalupe Garcia McCall, All American Boys and Ghost by Jason Reynolds, and I Am Not Your Perfect Mexican Daughter by Erika L. Sanchez. A delightful book to share with "kids from one to ninety-two" is The Day the Crayons Quit. Each of us can relate to the clever, humorous manner in which the author, Drew Daywalt, allows the crayons to voice their opinions about conflicts that exist in the crayon box--or in any situation "where two or more are gathered."

I have fond memories of enjoying reading times with my own children. Mary was a Strawberry Shortcake and Care Bear kid. I laughed a lot with Berlin while we read And I Mean It, Stanley by Crosby Bonsall. Not sure if he or I loved the book more, but either way we had fun with it. Reesha loved Dr. Seuss's Green Eggs and Ham and for a couple of years carried the book everywhere she went. I read it; she read it; we read it! There was an evening when I was on administrative duty at Bowie High School in Austin. I carried Reesha, a first grader, with me to the girls' basketball games. The junior varsity team members had finished their game and were watching the varsity game. After I returned to the gym from checking on other parts of the building, I found the junior varsity team members taking turns listening and reading Green Eggs and Ham to Reesha over and over again as I had done so many times before. The players were having a ball, and Reesha loved every ounce of attention that she was getting.

Students like to read and discuss books about heroes, such as Martin's Big Words: The Life of Dr. Martin Luther King, Jr. by Doreen Rappaport and Harvesting Hope: The Story of Cesar Chavez by Kathleen Krull. These two awarding winning books are great for compare-contrast discussions. Books about sports and entertainment figures are also very popular with school-aged children and should be available to them. Crossover, a Newbery Award winning novel by Kwame Alexander, is such a book because it includes rap and poetry for style and format, basketball for high interest, sibling rivalry, family loss, growing up, and many other real-life issues. For younger children, some favorites are Just Like Josh Gibson by Angela Johnson, Testing the Ice by Sharon Robinson, Jackie Robinson's sister, and The Bat Boy and His Violin by Gavin Curtis that combines baseball and music with family dynamics. When studying content from other subjects, discussions of books with the same topics help with making connections. The War That Saved My Life by Kimberly B. Bradley is an excellent book for supporting social studies discussions. The narrative presents both World War II and physical disability topics through the eyes of a ten-year old girl. Pink and Say by Patricia Polacco is a poignant children's book to use as an introduction to a unit on the Civil War. The main characters are 15-year-old boys fighting a war about which neither can make any sense. Bones by Steve Jenkins is a book with amazing photographs to support a science unit on skeletal systems.

Students in dance and other performing groups share my admiration of Misty Copeland and what she has accomplished by being the first and only African American principal ballerina for the American Ballet Theatre. Add a video of one of her performances to an excerpt from her autobiography, Life in Motion: An Unlikely Ballerina, and young, aspiring performers and others are hooked. They are eager to learn more about how her life changed from "being almost homeless" living with her family in a motel room to becoming the top performer in the competitive world of ballet. My husband, Johnny, and I had the pleasure of seeing her extraordinary performance in The Nutcracker at the Segerstrom Center for the Arts in Costa Mesa, California. Also, we met Misty backstage, which was "the icing on the cake."

In assessment, and certainly in instruction, what would students accomplish if they were engaged in more reading experiences that they found interesting and appealing?

Students, like adults, enjoy and excel in reading about subjects with which they can identify. I suppose that is why one of my favorite books is Preaching to the Chickens: The Story of Young John Lewis by Jabari Asim. The author and the illustrator depict delightful scenes of the farm on which John Lewis lived while growing up. This book brings back vivid memories of my own years growing up on a cotton farm in Northeast Texas with chickens, turkeys, and guineas running around all over the backyard. I love Cynthia Rylant's The Day the Relatives Came because this book reminds me of the summers when our relatives from West Texas came to visit us on the farm. Sometimes two carloads of relatives came to recreate "the good old days," hug a lot, eat a lot, and generate new energy and life for our farming world.

Books and materials are presented in many formats and styles, addressing a multitude of topics. Allowing students to choose books and materials that interest them causes higher amounts of reading and, subsequently, increases reading achievement. The more students engage in reading, the more their proficiency increases, just as the more that athletes practice a sport, the better they perform when playing the sport. Reading is too important to ignore. Frederick Douglass captured the importance in his quote, "Once you learn to read, you will be forever free."

Taking steps to involve students in enjoyable reading will lead to greater proficiency and increased reading achievement, eliminating the question of "Why can't they read?" When students have positive experiences with literacy beginning in the early stages of life, they are more successful in mastering the skills needed for reading and writing proficiency.

I have had the privilege of attending workshops and presentations delivered by experts throughout the country. I have met many giants in education and in reading, specifically. I acquired many effective reading strategies from experts, such as Anita Archer, Jo Robinson, Shane Templeton, Timothy Rasinki, Barry Lane, Donalyn Miller, Katherine Mitchell, Phyllis C. Hunter, Stephanie Harvey, Richard Allington, Lee Wright, Kelly Gallagher, Alfred Tatum, Douglas Fisher, Robert Slavin, Bill Blokker, and others. From them, the common theme is that purposeful interactions in literacy--engaging activities, explicit instruction, wide exposure to books, and independent reading--form the best route to increasing reading proficiency. Children can read when provided the proper support!

I have loved reading for as long as I can remember, and I am happy that my experiences on the farm only served to encourage me in that aspect of my life. While growing up in Northeast Texas, reading and learning were exciting and as important as the land itself. Visits back to our farm reignite memories of all the exciting and happy times on the land that my family and I had during the early years of my life.

PART III

BACK TO THE FARM

FOREVER THE LAND

The well-traveled roads are the same
The country store is still sitting there;
The village church is nestled amongst the old oak trees
The gate swings open wide to pasture space to spare.

So what's different?

There are no fields of cotton or corn
The house stands strong against the forces of time, but
No one is cooking in the warm and cozy little kitchen, and --
There's no aroma of bacon, coffee perking, and ham to cut.

No wildflower scents wafting through the evening air
No birds sitting in the trees chirping and cooing.
Where are the white sheets flapping in the wind?
Where are the distant sounds of cows mooing?

There is no clang of axes chopping aging wood
There's no fireplace flame to roast the peanuts just right
No one to complain about everything, argue or laugh with
And no one cultivating the land until there's no more light.

So what's left?

Oh, the memories are still there clear in the mind's eye
Memories of laughter from a big family and an extra girl or boy,
Melancholy moments listening to silence in a clear, moonlit night
Watching fireflies dance and stars frolic across the sky full of joy.

A legacy of dedication and determination of purpose
A lingering treasure of happiness and genuine love;
A land that spreads comforting blankets of warmth, security, and
A lifetime of pride with gratitude to the Father above.

c. j. brown

CHAPTER FOURTEEN

THIS LAND IS STILL OUR LAND

Stepping onto our land years later is a big reminder of what life there used to be: a white house with a red roof; long rows of cotton; chickens in the backyard; family get-togethers; reminiscing under the stars on hot summer nights; long bus rides to school; and so much more. So much is the same. On the other hand, many things are different. Many beloved people have gone on, but the land and many memories of life on the land still stand. The journey from the cotton farm in Northeast Texas to being an educator in several capacities and in several urban environments was exciting, rewarding, and fulfilling. There were also challenges along the way. However, it is a path that I am grateful I was able to take.

My parents, Berlin and Katherine Reese, and my oldest brother, Billy, are resting in heaven. I am sure they are happy that we still own and value the land. In order to be an everlasting part of the farm that was ours, Billy's remains are scattered in a pasture along the west side of the house where a green John Deere tractor sat during the time when crops were growing in the fields. Only one of my father's siblings remains alive. Dr. Calvin Reese, Daddy's youngest brother, lives in Houston, and leaves the care of my grandfather's land to my youngest brother, Frederick. Uncle Calvin celebrated his ninety-fifth birthday on December 18, 2020. Joan and he share the same birthdate. None of my mother's sisters or brothers are still with us.

There were three tracts of land purchased by my parents, Berlin and Katherine Reese, Essex Reese, my uncle, and my grandfather, Matt Reese. Almost seventy years later the Reeses still own all three tracts of the property. Michael, the fourth child, lives in the white house on the property that our parents, Berlin and Katherine Reese, purchased many years ago in 1952. The house is still a white house, but the red roof is gone. Michael maintains the remodeled house and the land even though there are only a few cattle and no crops.

Frederick and his wife, Deborah, live on the tract of land that my grandfather purchased. They built a beautiful house on the home site, making the place look like a replica of the mighty Ponderosa from the Bonanza television series--I tell them. They own the home site and six acres of land, but they care for the entire tract of more than 100 acres because they find the work relaxing. They care for a small herd of cattle and a horse named Susie that roam the pastures surrounding their home. Frederick and Deborah, with Michael's help, repair fences, feed cows, and shred pastures for relaxation. They say, "It's a hobby, and we enjoy doing it."

The third tract of land that Uncle Essex bought still remains with my cousin, Jane, Sister Maggie's and his only child.

I often thought about gaining employment in an air-conditioned building when I was younger and the sun was very hot without a cloud in sight. Now I cherish the work that I did on the farm because I contributed, in a small way, to building a treasure that transcended my own discomfort. Ownership of land is not just having a possession but is a part of a legacy that can be passed down through generations. I have very fond and lasting memories of growing up on the farm that my parents nurtured and left behind for us and for those who will follow.

In recent visits to the farm with my own family, I have walked with our children--Berlin, Mary, and Reesha--on parts of the land that were used for cattle and cotton crops. We took the same paths that I traveled years ago from house to fields and back again. As they looked at the property and captured the scenery through photography, I tried to convey some of what life was like when we were growing up there and the place was alive with crops, cattle, farm machines, and people who were family, relatives, friends, church members, and miscellaneous others who just happened to stop by because they knew they were always welcome.

I let Berlin, Mary, and Reesha know that the land was more than a possession to me and my family, but more important than my own thoughts about it, I hoped that the land would be a source of importance to them. Land can be a solid anchor that holds the heart and soul together forever. I know my sister and brothers--Joan, Michael, Frederick, and Billy, before he passed away--feel as I do about the legacy that our parents began many years ago. Our father and mother began this journey with love and determination, leaving behind memories that we all treasure and hold dear to our hearts. I am grateful for the chance to share my memories of life on the land in Northeast Texas with others, especially our children. My story is now a story for them and for others in their generation and for generations to come.

APPENDIX

Reading Visuals

Box It Up! - A visual to use for comparing two sets of vocabulary words from one or more selections. The visual can be used before or after reading. A sample copy is included. Grades 3-7.

WHY, WHAT--Causes and Effects – The cause-effect visual helps students to see relationships between events in a selection. Grades 3-7.

Eggs'iting Writing – This is a visual that asks students to take one vocabulary word and think of more colorful terms and uses for the original word. This exercise promotes thinking of ways to add excitement to literacy work. Grades 5-11.

2-Faced Fun – A visual that is designed for analyzing by comparing two characters from a selection by depicting their similarities and differences both verbally and visually. Grades 5-11.

4-Plan – Students work individually or as a team to analyze a portion of a selection—or a poem, picture, or short passage--by finding text evidence of key literary elements. This activity works well with teams using markers and large sheets of paper. The terms can be adapted depending on the selection. A sample is included. Grades 5-11.

More visuals and reading support materials can be found at J&C Brown Institute for Learning.

http://jcbil.com or **desire-to-aspire.com.**

Box It Up!

Place key vocabulary words from each topic in the box indicated.

WORDS:

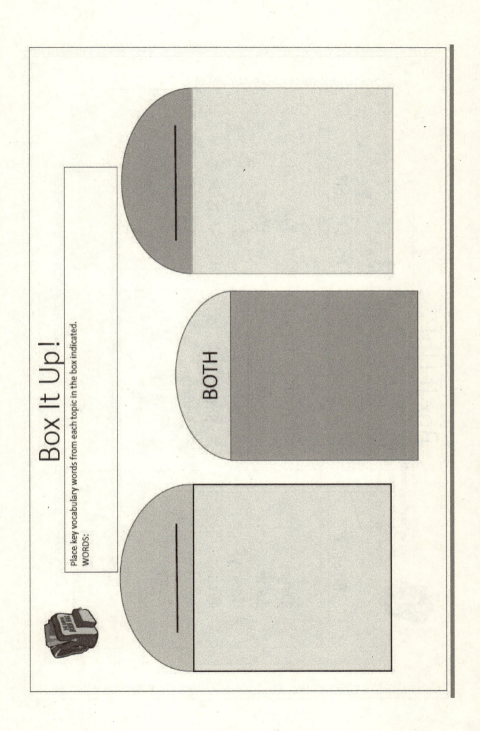

BOTH

Box It Up!

Place key vocabulary words from each topic in the box indicated.
WORDS: tee lane inside alley balls strike turkey holes course shoes outside sports birdie rivalry pins clubs three

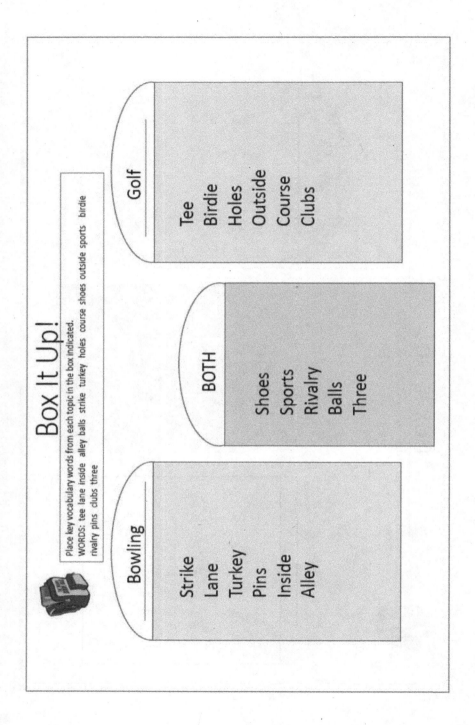

Bowling	BOTH	Golf
Strike	Shoes	Tee
Lane	Sports	Birdie
Turkey	Rivalry	Holes
Pins	Balls	Outside
Inside	Three	Course
Alley		Clubs

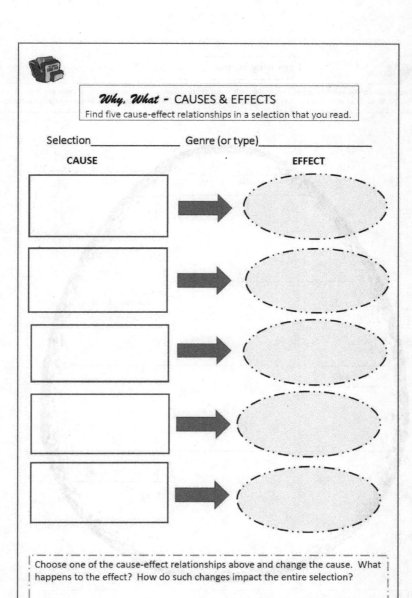

Why, What - CAUSES & EFFECTS
Find five cause-effect relationships in a selection that you read.

Selection_____ Genre (or type)_____

CAUSE   **EFFECT**

Choose one of the cause-effect relationships above and change the cause. What happens to the effect? How do such changes impact the entire selection?

Eggs'iting Writing

I. Teacher (or another leader) chooses a vocabulary word—verb or noun, and for each section think of other words as indicated. Work as an individual or rotate through a team of four. The original owner completes Part II and decorates the egg.

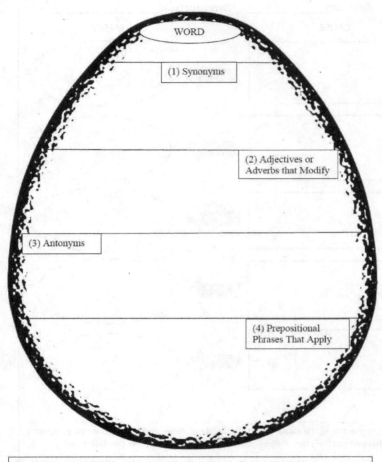

WORD

(1) Synonyms

(2) Adjectives or Adverbs that Modify

(3) Antonyms

(4) Prepositional Phrases That Apply

II. Write a sentence using at least one word, or phrase, from each section.

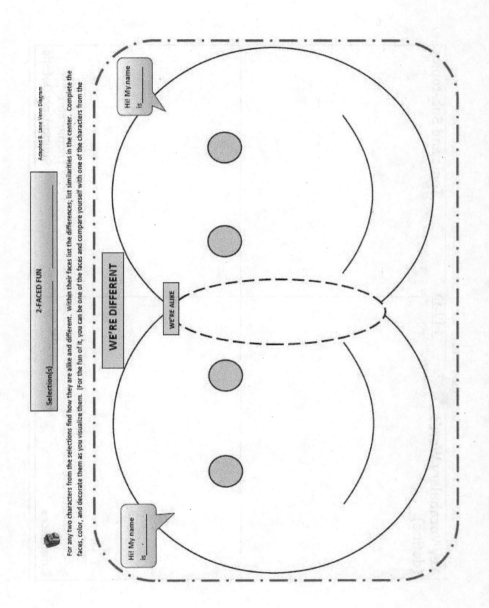

Selection(s) _____

2-FACED FUN

Adapted B. Lane Venn Diagram

For any two characters from the selections find how they are alike and different. Within their faces list the differences; list similarities in the center. Complete the faces, color, and decorate them as you visualize them. (For the fun of it, you can be one of the faces and compare yourself with one of the characters from the

WE'RE DIFFERENT

WE'RE ALIKE

Hi! My name is _____

Hi! My name is _____

Key Vocabulary Words (define)

4-PLAN

(Use selection you read to complete the 4 parts of this chart.)

Topic and Sub-topics

Theme and Supporting Details

Inferences

Key Vocabulary Word
(define)

Government – political system that administers and regulates a country, city, or state

Shutdown – closure of an organization, usually temporarily

Workers – people employed to complete specific tasks

4-PLAN
(Use selection you read to complete the 4 parts of this chart.)

Topic and Sub-topics

- Closure of government offices
- Loss of jobs
- Process for making gvt. budgets

Editorial   Political Cartoon

NEXT GOVERNMENT SHUTDOWN

YOU GET USED TO IT.

GOV'T WORKER

Inferences

1. One worker has experience working in this office
2. Same worker has been unemployed and returned to work several times before
3. Second worker is new to the job
4. Second worker is fearful of losing job
5. Closing government offices often occurs until budget is approved

Theme:
Experience reduces worry

Details:
1. Uncertain budget for government
2. Possible shutdown
3. Threat of job loss generates fear - knife
4. Having gone through loss makes it less threatening – you get used to it

Theme and Supporting Details

REFERENCES

Brown, J. E. (2020). *The Emerson Street story: Race, class, quality of life and faith*. Bloomington, IN: AuthorHouse.

Dias, M. (2018). *Marley Dias gets it done, and so can you!* New York: Scholastic Press.

Fisher, D. & Frey, N. (2018). *Rigorous reading: 5 access points for comprehending complex texts*. Thousand Oaks, CA: Sage Publications Ltd.

Green, V. H. (1940). *The Negro motorist green-book*. New York City, NY: Victor H. Green.

Harvill, D. (2020). Aikin, A. M. Jr. *Handbook of Texas online* (October 02, 2020). Retrieved from https://www.tshaonline.org/handbook/entries/aikin-a-m-jr

Hunter, P. C. (2012). *It's not complicated! What I know for sure about helping our students of color become successful readers*. New York, NY: Scholastic.

Jett, B. (2013). Paris is burning: Lynching and racial violence in Lamar County, 1890-1920. *East Texas Historical Journal*, 51, 40-64. Scholarworks.sfasu.edu/ethj/vol51/iss2/9

Kamkwamba, W. & Mealer, B. (2015). *The boy who harnessed the wind*. New York, NY: Dial Books for Young Readers.

McNamara. R. (2020). *"1893 Lynching by fire of Henry Smith.* ThoughtCo, August 26, 2020. Thoughtco.com/1893-lynching-of-henry-smith-4082215

Schmoker, M. (2011). *Focus: Elevating the essentials to radically improve student learning.* Alexandria, VA: ASCD.

Tatum, A. (2005). *Teaching reading to black adolescent males: Closing the achievement gap.* Portland, MN: Stenhouse Publishers.

Vaughan, D. (1977, May 25). Katherine Reese: 24 years of school. *The Paris News.* pp. 18, 2B.

Carolyn J. Brown

Carolyn Jean (Reese) Brown grew up on a farm in Northeast Texas--Paris (Lamar County). Her early education occurred at Powderly High School in a small community north of Paris. Carolyn graduated and received degrees from Paris Junior College, the University of North Texas, and the University of Texas at Austin. She continued her graduate studies at Texas State University and Texas A&M - Commerce and was an educator in four different states. Carolyn retired after fifty years of employment. She continues to share her professional knowledge and skills through volunteering in the community. She and her husband, Dr. Johnny E. Brown, live in Port Arthur, Texas, and they attend Antioch Missionary Baptist Church in Beaumont. They have three children, two sons-in-law, and one granddaughter.